ANTHROPOLOGY

ANTHROPOLOGY

Edited by
Allan H. Smith and John L. Fischer

A SPECTRUM BOOK

Prentice-Hall, Inc., *Englewood Cliffs, N. J.*

Prentice-Hall International, Inc. (*London*)
Prentice-Hall of Australia, Pty. Ltd. (*Sydney*)
Prentice-Hall of Canada, Ltd. (*Toronto*)
Prentice-Hall of India Private Limited (*New Delhi*)
Prentice-Hall of Japan, Inc. (*Tokyo*)

FOREWORD

This book is one of a series prepared in connection with the Survey of the Behavioral and Social Sciences conducted between 1967 and 1969 under the auspices of the Committee on Science and Public Policy of the National Academy of Sciences and the Problems and Policy Committee of the Social Science Research Council.

The Survey provides a comprehensive review and appraisal of these rapidly expanding fields of knowledge, and constitutes a basis for an informed, effective national policy to strengthen and develop these fields even further.

The reports in the Survey, each the work of a panel of scholars, include studies of anthropology, economics, geography, history as a social science, political science, psychology, psychiatry as a behavioral science, sociology, and the social science aspects of statistics, mathematics and computation. A general volume discusses relations among the disciplines, broad questions of utilization of the social sciences by society, and makes specific recommendations for public and university policy.

While close communication among all concerned has been the rule, individual panel reports are the responsibility of the panels producing them. They have not been formally reviewed or approved by the Central Planning Committee or by the sponsoring organizations. They were reviewed at an earlier stage by representatives of the National Academy of Sciences and the Social Science Research Council.

Much of the data on the behavioral and social sciences in universities used in these reports comes from a 1968 questionnaire survey, conducted by the Survey Committee, of universities offering the PhD in one of these fields. Questionnaires were filled out by

PhD-granting departments (referred to as the Departmental Questionnaire); by selected professional schools (referred to as the Professional School Questionnaire); by computation centers (referred to as the Computation Center Questionnaire); by financial offices (referred to as the Administration Questionnaire); and by research institutes, centers, laboratories and museums engaged in research in the behavioral and social sciences (referred to as the Institute Questionnaire). Further information concerning this questionnaire survey is provided in the appendix to the general report of the Central Planning Committee, *The Behavioral and Social Sciences: Outlook and Needs* (Englewood Cliffs, N.J.: Prentice-Hall, Inc., 1969).

Also included in the appendix of the report of the Central Planning Committee is a discussion of the method of degree projection used in these reports, as well as some alternative methods.

THE BEHAVIORAL AND SOCIAL SCIENCES SURVEY COMMITTEE
CENTRAL PLANNING COMMITTEE

Ernest R. Hilgard, *Stanford University*, CHAIRMAN
Henry W. Riecken, *Social Science Research Council*, CO-CHAIRMAN
Kenneth E. Clark, *University of Rochester*
James A. Davis, *Dartmouth College*
Fred R. Eggan, *The University of Chicago*
Heinz Eulau, *Stanford University*
Charles A. Ferguson, *Stanford University*
John L. Fischer, *Tulane University of Louisiana*
David A. Hamburg, *Stanford University*
Carl Kaysen, *Institute for Advanced Study*
William H. Kruskal, *The University of Chicago*
David S. Landes, *Harvard University*
James G. March, *University of California, Irvine*
George A. Miller, *The Rockefeller University*
Carl Pfaffmann, *The Rockefeller University*
Neil J. Smelser, *University of California, Berkeley*
Allan H. Smith, *Washington State University*
Robert M. Solow, *Massachusetts Institute of Technology*
Edward Taaffe, *The Ohio State University*
Charles Tilly, *The University of Michigan*
Stephen Viederman, *National Academy of Sciences*, EXECUTIVE OFFICER

CONTENTS

ANTHROPOLOGY

PREFACE

This report represents the cooperative efforts of a panel of eight anthropologists, appointed in late 1966 by the National Academy of Sciences and the Social Science Research Council to undertake, under their joint auspices, one of the series of studies which comprise the Behavioral and Social Sciences Survey (BASS). The primary general goal of the report is to provide a balanced statement of the past accomplishments, present status, and future prospects of anthropology. Hopefully, it will prove useful to those governmental and private agencies which support anthropology, to federal and state legislators and other potential users of anthropological knowledge, to university administrators who can influence anthropology's future development in the academic context, and to the general public whose concerns are increasingly spoken to by anthropology. The report is secondarily designed to present an informative overview of the field for nonanthropological professionals, for students, and for interested laymen.

Through the months the panel met on many occasions to design the structure of the report, to plan data gathering and compilation procedures, and to define the special issues to which particular attention should be given and the postures which it wished to take in regard to them.

In assembling this report a rich body of resource data was gathered. Published and manuscript data summaries and syntheses were solicited from many colleagues. Current publications in anthropology were combed for relevant material. With the assistance of the Survey

1

Committee staff, government and other statistical studies were examined for information concerning the field and the demographic characteristics of anthropologists. Following the previously agreed upon plan, the individual chapters and chapter sections were then written by individual panel members. The whole was assembled, reviewed, and edited by all panel members.

The report is selective, not exhaustive. Nevertheless, it attempts a great deal: it suggests the scope of the discipline by illustrating what some anthropologists have done; it indicates the history and major accomplishments of each of the principal subfields; it describes the interrelationships of these subfields and the interlocking interests of anthropology and tangent disciplines; it defines some of the frontiers of anthropology; it surveys current and anticipated personnel and facilities needs; it projects in a tentative manner anthropology's probable development over the coming few years; and it formulates a series of recommendations to improve the discipline and increase its usefulness in applied contexts. In keeping with the orientation of the Survey, special emphasis is given to the ways in which anthropology has contributed to the understanding, and even solution, of urgent social and economic problems, to some of the practical and ethical difficulties which confront anthropologists in applying their knowledge, and to the future of applied anthropology. The report makes an effort to present not only the achievements and strengths of anthropology but also, quite candidly, certain of its more perplexing weaknesses and limitations. Since its net is cast so widely, the report treats none of these subjects in more than a summary fashion. Many important data are totally omitted: a number of well recognized subfields are not even mentioned. Specific illustrations of general propositions are kept to a minimum. In short, the report is only a survey and makes no pretense to being more.

Probably no member of the panel finds this report fully satisfactory or can endorse the whole without some reservations. Some would have preferred more detail or less emphasis on a particular point, the inclusion of a new subject or the deletion of data presently discussed, a different interpretation, or a more or less cautious prediction. In the final writing, some of the more suggestive material was trimmed, particularly findings in regard to the current status of the discipline and panel opinions about the probable future of anthropology and how it might best chart its course. Nevertheless, as a joint product, the report is supported in its present form by all panel members.

It is important to view this summary as an extension of the general survey, *The Behavioral and Social Sciences: Outlook and Needs.* This broader survey examines the common characteristics and requirements of the social sciences as a whole and proposes a set of general recommendations. This overview of anthropology alone places these statements in sharper focus in terms of this particular discipline and, in addition, calls attention to the specific and peculiar features, needs, and prospects of anthropology.

The Anthropology Panel was initially organized with Sherwood Washburn as Chairman and Allan H. Smith as Co-Chairman. When Washburn found it necessary to resign due to the press of other duties, Smith became Chairman and J. L. Fischer replaced Smith as Co-Chairman. Washburn continued as a member of the Panel until the completion of its work.

The assistance of a very large number of anthropological colleagues must be acknowledged. Those who responded with copies of their manuscripts and recent summary papers are far too numerous to list, but to them the panel is very grateful. Others contributed more heavily in various ways: Angel Palerm, J. O. Brew, Fred R. Eggan, Stanley M. Garn, Eugene Giles, John V. Murra, and particularly George M. Foster, Jr., who, though not a panel member, authored one section of the report. Charles Frantz, formerly executive secretary of the American Anthropological Association, and Margaret Fallers provided especially useful information. The chairmen of many departments of anthropology and other university administrators contributed in 1968 questionnaire data of basic importance to an understanding of the needs and costs of the discipline within the academic structure. It is a special pleasure to recognize the panel's indebtedness to Ernest R. Hilgard and Henry W. Riecken, Co-Chairmen of the Survey Committee, and to Stephen Viederman, the committee's executive officer, for their forbearance and highly perceptive guidance from the beginning of the project to its close. In addition, the members of the Central Planning Committee furnished the general orientation and structure of the report. Likewise the panel is also grateful to the four members of the review panel who studied the manuscript in its draft form and made many thoughtful suggestions for its improvement: Cora Du Bois, Bentley Glass, Fred P. Thieme, and Robert Fogel. The panel received a number of helpful comments on the draft of the report from Howard H. Hines and Richard Lieban of the National Science Foundation. Nevertheless, the final report is that of the panel authors and they must bear the onus for its imperfections. Finally, the panel wishes to express its deep appreciation to the Russell Sage Foundation, the National Institutes of Health, the National Institute of Mental Health, and the National Science Foundation for the funding which made the study possible.

1
THE CONCERNS OF ANTHROPOLOGY

Anthropology deals with the origin, development, and nature of man and his culture. It differs from other social sciences in its comparative approach, studying man today and in the past, as part of Western civilization and in cultures unlike our own. From its perspective, its awareness of the range of cultural similarities and differences, it searches for the common denominators of human existence and the forces that condition persistence or change in customs or whole cultures. The anthropologist is always concerned with the relevance of his work to the total contemporary world.

During the past half-century, anthropologists have been most prominently concerned with the direct study of relatively small societies and cultures—tribes, villages, or localized minorities, for example. Attention has often been directed to nonliterate cultures, that is, to small groups that have no written records and therefore transmit their culture directly through the spoken word or through their institutional arrangements. This kind of activity, important as it has been in developing an understanding of the range of human institutionalized behavior, encompasses only a small part of anthropology. But it does help to make the field recognizably different from closely related behavioral sciences like psychology—which is usually more concerned with individual behavior—and sociology—which tends to work with the structures of more "advanced" societies like the modern industrial nations. Darwin's influence on anthropology was strong, so that it is concerned with the biological evolution of man as well

5

as with early cultures and cultural evolution. Rather than entering immediately into a structured examination of the nature of anthropology, this introductory chapter will describe a few typical problems of human biology and human behavior that have fascinated anthropologists, that represent distinctively anthropological lines of inquiry, and that have led to anthropological findings of interest. Together, these examples are intended to be an illustration of the scope and dimensions of the discipline—incomplete, to be sure, but having the advantage of concreteness.

THE ORIGINS OF NEW WORLD CIVILIZATION

In February, 1960, after several years of intensive archaeological investigation both to the north and south of Mexico City, Richard MacNeish and several local guides scrambled into a small rock-sheltered cave near the village of Coxcatlan in the southern part of the valley of Tehuacán. They had already investigated thirty-eight different caves in the area without success. But in the Coxcatlan cave six primitive corncobs were discovered, dated by subsequent carbon 14 analyses at 5,600 years in age—500 years older than any previously found in the New World. The discovery of corncobs of such antiquity immediately raised questions as to whether this was the area where corn had first been domesticated and thus where New World civilization had been born.

Scientists and laymen alike had for centuries been interested in how and why civilizations develop. What, for instance, is the process involved in the transition from a small, loosely organized, relatively homogeneous band of hunters and gatherers to a much larger, more complex group occupying cities and towns and engaging in those political and religious activities that have come to be associated with the attainment of civilization? It has been widely held that the single most significant occurrence in human history was the development of agriculture and animal husbandry, precisely because these activities are believed to have provided the foundation for the transition from "savagery" to "civilization." Through the domestication of plants and animals, man was able to achieve some degree of independence from the nomadic life of the hunter and gatherer. The people of the Old

World transformed their native grasses into wheat, barley, and oats, but maize was the only important wild grass in the New World to be transformed into a food grain. Because of the dominance of this plant in New World agriculture, prehistorians have long been confident that if they could discover when, where, and under what circumstances it was first domesticated, they might also uncover the origins of New World civilization.

It became apparent that if the wide-ranging implications of Mac-Neish's discovery at Coxcatlan were to be fully realized, the final stages of the investigation would require the knowledge and expertise of scientists from a wide variety of disciplines, not only archaeology and botany. The project eventually engaged some fifty specialists, among them zoologists, geologists, and ethnographers.

The key to the valley's prehistoric cultural development lay with the anthropologically trained archaeologists, however, and before the project was completed twelve archaeological sites had been excavated in the valley of Tehuacán. The Coxcatlan cave, where the work had begun, turned out to be the richest. It yielded twenty-eight separate occupation levels, the earliest of which may date to about 10,000 B.C. These findings, in combination with the data from Purron Cave, which contained twenty-five floors dating from about 7,000 B.C. to 500 B.C., provide an almost continuous record of nearly 12,000 years of prehistory, by far the longest record for any New World area.

In four seasons of digging and archaeological survey (from 1961 through 1964) the project team reaped a vast archaeological harvest. Because of the extreme dryness of the area, in more than fifty-five of the floors in the five caves everything had been preserved: foods, feces, and other normally perishable human remains and artifacts. Nearly a million individual remains of human activity were recovered, along with more than 1,000 animal bones (including those of extinct antelopes and horses), 80,000 individual wild-plant remains, and some 25,000 specimens of corn, even though only five caves contained maize remains. Using the valley's geology and the shells of its land snails, pollen and other plant parts, and a variety of other remains from the excavations, the specialists traced the changes in climate, physical environment, and plant and animal life during the 12,000-year time span during which man lived in Tehuacán. For the archaeologists, the refuse from these caves permits an unusually complete reconstruction of the way of life of the ancient inhabitants and hence a nearly continuous picture of the rise of civilization in the valley of Tehuacán. From the kinds of plant remains in various occupation levels, the specialists even determined at what seasons of the year many of the floors in the caves were occupied.

It appears that the Tehuacanos lived for thousands of years as nomadic collectors of wild vegetable and animal foods before they made their first timid efforts at agriculture. It was during the phase following their life in the Coxcatlan cave that they made this fundamental subsistence shift. By about 3,400 B.C. the food provided by agriculture rose to approximately 30 per cent of the total diet, domesticated animals (starting with the dog) made their appearance, and the first fixed settlements, small pit-house villages, were formed. By this time, the Abejas period, the people lived at a subsistence level that can be regarded as a foundation for the beginning of civilization.

It can be said that the people of Tehuacán are the first whose evolution from primitive food collectors to civilized agriculturists has been traced in detail. As yet we have no such complete story either for the Old World or for other parts of the New World. We also have at Tehuacán evidence of the earliest village life in the New World and also the first pottery in Mexico and a relatively large sample of some of the earliest Indian skeletons yet known. But more important, the Tehuacán material at last provides one New World example of the development of a society from savagery to civilization. Preliminary analyses of these data indicate that the traditional hypothesis about the evolution of high cultures may have to be reexamined and modified, for the characteristic elements of the Neolithic revolution fail to appear suddenly in the form of a new culture complex or a revolutionized way of life.

WHAT CAN BE LEARNED FROM ARTIFACTS OF ANCIENT CIVILIZATIONS

A problem that has continually confronted anthropologists—archaeologists and ethnographers alike—has been that of reliably recreating the social milieu of prehistoric societies. How, for instance, does one make sound statements about the social organization of kinship patterns of now extinct groups? How can the nature and duration of intragroup contact and interaction, or the level of group cohesiveness, be discovered for a selected prehistoric society? Unfortunately, these and many other aspects of extinct cultural systems are not directly reflected in the material objects recovered through site excavation. Therefore, they have commonly fallen outside the subject areas that prehistorians have been able to cope with, so that much of archaeology's contribution to the general field of anthropology has traditionally centered in the areas of description, taxonomy, and inventories of stylistic traits.

In recent years, however, many archaeologists have become increasingly interested in restructuring the traditional focus of the field so that verifiable anthropological inferences might be made from an examination of prehistoric material objects. An undertaking designed to develop just such an approach was William Longacre's attempt to demonstrate a correlation between social organization and residence on the one hand and the distribution of ceramic design attributes on the other.

The Longacre project illustrates the possibilities of reclaiming sociological information from sources long neglected by archaeologists. It was hoped that a detailed analysis of ceramic designs in a selected prehistoric site would provide information about social groupings. Underlying this approach was the assumption that the smaller and more closely tied the social groups, the more details of design would be shared. It was further assumed that, since social demography and social organization are reflected in the material objects of a cultural system, social demography in a matrilineal, matrilocal society might be mirrored in the ceramic art of female potters. The smaller and more closely tied these matrilineal social aggregates, the more details of design would be shared.

The Carter Ranch site in a long and relatively narrow valley east of Snowflake, Arizona was chosen to test the approach. To supplement the data recovered from this site, an intensive archaeological survey of the entire valley was carried out and a large collection of artifacts was taken from each site. In addition, valleys to the north and east of the site were also surveyed; on the basis of field analysis one other site was also selected for partial excavation.

After the initial excavation and surface collection from surrounding valleys, a usable sample was drawn from the more than 15,000 decorated sherds (pieces of broken pottery) recovered. Because of the wealth of artifacts obtained, only black-on-white sherds were studied and only those sherds which had at least one complete element of design.

The results of the analysis were exciting. They showed that the design elements and element groups were definitely nonrandom in their distribution: the probability of the demonstrated distribution occurring with such consistency due to chance alone was about one in a million. Plotting the design elements on distribution maps revealed that certain pottery types tended to be consistently associated with particular types of rooms: e.g., with ceremonial units like kivas. Moreover, a high correlation between pottery types and room *features* suggested a series of functionally specific room types which combined as structural units to form the pueblo as a whole.

Data from the architectural analysis of the site and the statistical analysis of the pottery-type distributions correlated with the clustering of design elements. For example, analysis of the sequence in which the rooms were built revealed two major construction areas, which were also associated with the element "cluster areas." Clearly as each area of construction expanded by the addition of new rooms, the rectangular pueblo was formed. This pattern of community growth is considered characteristic of recent Western Pueblo construction. As daughters marry, the localized matrilineage maintains its spatial corporateness by adding rooms to the original household to accommodate the increase in the number of family members.

Vessels similar in design to the ceremonial ones were also associated with burials, suggesting graveside ritual.

The evidence of the Carter Ranch site suggests that the prehistoric pueblo was occupied by two localized lineages, the actual areas occupied by them being reflected in the design element clustering. Furthermore, the pottery association of these elements strongly suggests that the descent groups were matrilineal and practiced matrilocal residence.

These findings attest to the value of utilizing in archaeological research a detailed design element analysis to retrieve sociological information that might otherwise be overlooked. An analysis of this kind permits a larger number of valid anthropological inferences, based upon the combining of systematic sampling procedures with traditional as well as new methods of data processing and computer analysis.

DO MEN OF DIFFERENT
CULTURES THINK ALIKE?

One of the achievements of anthropology has been to provide new insights into the minds of men who live in ways far different from our own. Working cooperatively with psychologists Seymour Sarason and Ulric Neisser, anthropologist Thomas Gladwin has recently discovered some significant facts about how men think— when their cultural backgrounds are very different. This perplexing question is of great practical as well as theoretical importance, for every year many children enter school with intellectual deficits in cultural background that doom them under our present educational system to frustration in school and menial jobs after they leave. Most, but not all, are children of poverty. Generations of researchers have documented the fact that their thinking is different, but little is known of *how* these children *do* think.

It occurred to Gladwin and Sarason that although their thinking might differ from American middle-class thinking, it could still be just as satisfactory for their purposes. Instead of testing this notion directly with the poor in this country, Gladwin chose to examine the thinking of a people who accomplish unmistakable intellectual feats with a thinking style that appeared to be just as concrete as that of our poor. In the central Caroline Islands of Micronesia, part of the United States Trust Territory, is the island of Puluwat, whose navigators are renowned throughout the Pacific for their skill. Setting sail for Satawal, an island 130 miles to the west, one-half mile long, they regularly reach their landfall with less than 10 miles error, a deviation of 4½ degrees. There are strong and unpredictable crosscurrents and no way of positively confirming their position en route. Gladwin argued that such accomplishments might be made without advance planning and with a different style of thinking from that which is familiar to us. The issue was of great theoretical importance as well, for Benjamin Whorf had suggested in a series of brilliant papers that the fundamental categories of thought in other cultures might be as unlike our own as was the syntax of Hopi. The Hopi language, for example, suggests a concept of "intensity of action"—the equivalent of our concept of rate, but not based on time. The possibility of differing types of thinking in other cultures intrigues and challenges anthropologists.

Seen in this context, Gladwin's findings are as startling as they are unequivocal. The Puluwat navigator thinks essentially as do successful navigators everywhere. He follows a system of dead reckoning that is known elsewhere, even though the details are not generalized but specific to the few hundreds of miles of ocean in which the system developed. He plots the direction of his travel by star courses, based upon the direction in which certain stars rise and set on the horizon. He keeps track of distance traveled by means of time elapsed and his detailed knowledge of the speed of his canoe under varying conditions. Much of this information is recorded in his mind in terms of a purely abstract conceptual model in which his canoe, and the star courses, are seen as motionless upon a sea dotted with unseen islands under their star courses, which flow by him at a rate determined by his estimate of his speed. None of his detailed plans calls for any innovation on his part. He learns all of the alternatives when he becomes a navigator. Even when blown off course, he does not need to formulate a wholly new plan: he merely sails until he hits a familiar "seamark," and then follows an old plan from there.

These findings add to a growing body of evidence that certain logical processes are universal. We no longer have to ask of another people how they think, but what they think about. They also provide a new perspective on the so-called "concrete" thinking of lower-income people in our own culture. It suddenly becomes apparent that such people can and do think abstractly as well as concretely. Invisible islands moving under star courses are abstract thoughts. A taxi driver negotiating a route through variable traffic accidents and construction obstacles in any big city is thinking like a Puluwat navigator: abstractly, but not innovatively. The irony is that on Puluwat the navigator is admired by everyone; but the taxi driver in the city is not. Better understanding of these thinking processes can lead to wiser educational practices and wiser vocational guidance.

EXPERIENCE AND PERCEPTION

The Kohs Block Test is sometimes used as an item in intelligence tests. It consists of a series of colored blocks, some with diagonal color divisions on their faces; these blocks have to be arranged to duplicate a printed pattern that the tester places before the person being tested.

This test is unusually difficult for African children and adults. It is a commonplace of anthropology that we see what we are taught to see, and the conjecture is that something in the experience of those raised in parts of Africa causes the difficulty with the test—not any deficiency in native intelligence.

Recently Roy D'Andrade conducted a series of experiments with the Kohs blocks in Nigeria and later repeated the experiments in Ghana. The children he tested had difficulties. A period of training in which children were given an opportunity to practice constructing Kohs block designs from diagrams produced no improvement. On retest, most still showed a marked inferiority to American and European children in carrying out the task, though a few of them caught on immediately.

D'Andrade was not content to leave the matter there. He examined the test material and discovered that 95 per cent of all mistakes occurred in placing block faces which require a diagonal color division, and that the failure came in orienting the diagonal properly. D'Andrade hoped to improve learning by simplifying the problem, but reducing the number of blocks used in the training sessions did little to improve results. Finally he hit upon the solution. The children continued to fail in the task so long as they were asked to copy a design from a drawing and reproduce it in blocks. If given another set of blocks, they had immediate success in producing a copy. The problem had been in the multiple discriminations necessary in going from a picture of a pattern to the actual arrangement of the blocks. The new training program, in which children were shown the relationship between blocks and diagram, quickly raised the level of performance to that normal for children in industrial societies.

The deficiency thus turned out to rest primarily on lack of familiarity with pictorial representation. In rural Hausa villages children rarely see pictures or drawings of any type. Even adults are baffled by maps or building diagrams. That the difficulties are accounted for by lack of experience with pictures rather than lack of intelligence was shown by D'Andrade's success in training children first to copy from a comparable set of blocks and then to match a diagram.

THE GOLDEN STOOL
AS A NATIONAL SYMBOL

Human communication is based on the ability to use symbols, and the ability to manipulate symbols lies behind all of our cultural achievements. But our very facility in this direction gives rise to most of the misunderstandings that plague human relationships, especially when we deal with one another across the boundaries of social experience. Symbols do not automatically signal their meanings to the onlooker or listener. He has to learn how to interpret what he sees and hears. Until he does so, he flounders from mistake to mistake as he tries to use his own culture to provide him with cues for understanding. British subjects are amazed that Americans respond with deep emotion to the burning of their flag, assuming that flag to carry the same symbolic stress as the Union Jack. In fact it is much more closely linked to emotions of national identity, which in Britain find expression in the symbols of crown and monarch rather than in the flag.

The classic case of misunderstanding of national symbols took place in the early days of British rule in West Africa. The colonial governor demanded that the Ashanti of central Ghana seat him upon the golden stool which he knew to be associated with their king. For him stool and chair were synonymous; the golden stool was presumed to be a throne and thus the appropriate seat for the representative of the imperial power. The Ashanti heard him out and rose in revolt, for in fact he had asked them to give him their national soul. As each individual Ashanti had a soul, so did the nation as a whole. When the golden stool first appeared, in the reign of the fourth king of Ashanti, it was announced as the repository of the soul of the Ashanti people "bound up with their power, their honor, their welfare, and that if it were captured or destroyed the nation would perish." The stool was the most sacred possession of the Ashanti. It was a national shrine under the guardianship of the king. It was never allowed to touch the ground. Certainly it could never be used as a throne. Revolt was probably the inevitable answer to the proposed desecration and the insult to Ashanti identity.

After months of fighting and the loss of many lives the revolt was put down, but the golden stool remained hidden away in the heart of Ashantiland. That the British administrators respected the stool when it was accidentally discovered some twenty years later lies to the credit of applied anthropology. In the interim the colonial administration had appointed Robert Rattray, a young anthropologist, to study Ashanti life in the hope that better understanding would lead to better administration. His studies are now classics of anthropology. He was able to explain the symbolic meaning of the stool so that it was clear what it meant to the Ashanti. His work demonstrated the importance of identifying and understanding the symbols in which different peoples define their national and personal identity. His research, though remote in time and space, had direct bearing on American practice after World War II when anthropologists and other social scientists urged that the United States respect the position and person of the Japanese emperor, who was the symbol of the Japanese nation and as such provided for the continuity of legitimate authority.

REBELLION ON THE COPPERBELT

The university crisis of the 1960s has parallels with the situation which confronted the Copperbelt in what was then Northern Rhodesia during the strikes of 1935 and 1940. Both involved a confrontation exacerbated by a dispute over the legitimacy of leadership.

In the 1930s the Copperbelt consisted of a number of very new mining towns that had recruited thousands of unskilled African workers from the surrounding territory. Many of the workers came hundreds of miles to work in what was a very new environment. They streamed into the towns as migrant laborers, unused to city life and unfamiliar with one another. Most of the European employees were equally new to central Africa, but at least they came from other industrial settings and brought with them the model for town organization.

The colonial government, recognizing the importance of African leadership, thought it was doing the right thing when it appointed senior men from each of the various tribes to serve as spokesmen for their fellows. During the first African strike in 1935, the European officials turned to these tribal elders, only to find that the tribal elders were fleeing to them for protection against their fellows.

The tribal elders were tied to a rural way of life no longer appropriate to the industrial community, and they had lost their authority in this setting. An effort was made to revitalize the links to the countryside through visits by important chiefs, which worked for a time, but in a later strike the "elders" were again pushed aside as irrelevant. A. L. Epstein, the anthropologist who studied the emerging African society of Luanshya in the late 1940s and early 1950s, argued that the town was a social setting and that anyone who came within its orbit found himself enmeshed in new sets of relationships that were distinct from those of the country. Urban life had to be coped with as a thing in itself.

The administration had not recognized the speed with which people respond to new situations and learn to segregate their various relationships; nor had they realized that leadership becomes situational. In dealing with the elders, who had only a limited role to play in urban life, as though they represented all the interests of the people living in town, the administration succeeded only in discrediting them and in slowing the emergence of responsible leadership linked to the variety of interests that African townsmen shared with one another.

ANTHROPOLOGY AND
THE INTELLECTUAL CLIMATE

The foregoing and somewhat fragmented picture of anthropologists going about their business by no means covers the whole field. The important subfields of physical anthropology and linguistic anthropology are not represented at all; they will be introduced later. Something of the flavor of what anthropologists do has been conveyed. Now attention can be directed to some of the larger intellectual contributions of anthropology.

Over the past century anthropologists have reached certain broad conclusions from the masses of observational and experimental data they have accumulated. One such conclusion is the conviction as to the essential intellectual equality of all large groups of mankind, irrespective of their biological characteristics. Supported by the data of other behavioral and social sciences, this conclusion must be seen as underlying recent social legislation and court judgments, such as those designed to promote the social equality of the races and the progress of integration in the United States.

Similarly, during the past hundred years anthropologists have been largely responsible for the development of the concept of "culture." By documenting the enormous range of cultural behavior in societies in all parts of the world; by studying societies under culture change, both internally generated and externally fostered; and by examining the process of cultural transmission from generation to generation, anthropologists have demonstrated beyond question that the precise structure of an individual's behavior is overwhelmingly the result of learning and is preponderantly determined by the cultural patterns of his group.

Anthropology has been deeply involved in documenting the relationship between the cultural practices of a society and the modal personality type characteristic of the members of that society. According to the premise fundamental to this approach, the experiences of early childhood, particularly those resulting from sanctioned training patterns and backed by rewards and punishments, exert a profound impact upon the developing child. In concert, they serve to establish in early life basic value orientations and normative responses to people, things, events, and the world around. The early field studies of Margaret Mead in the Pacific, now well known, were directed in part toward illuminating the consequences of the patterned experiences of childhood on the personality of the adolescent and adult. The broad conclusions of this block of studies have found their way into the fundamental postulates of many who, through their popular writings, have over recent years exercised a major influence on childrearing practices in our society.

Far more than any other discipline, anthropology has established the nature and significance of the diversity of man, both physically and in learned cultural and speech behavior. Anthropology's scientifically verified data have served to combat the many, and sometimes dangerous, misconceptions and half-truths that continue to emerge from the field observations and theoretical speculations of the anthropologically untrained. Neither the genocidal theories of Hitler nor the fanciful Voltairian notions of a primitive Elysian state, the biblical doctrine of man's creation nor the ill-boding predictions of contemporary railers against interracial marriages receive support in the findings of anthropology. But more than this, anthropology gives a new sense of man's abilities to cope with his environment, often enough limited in resources and rigorous in the extreme; of his extraordinary inventiveness; of the great range of his psychological adaptability; and of his potential for further development in whatever directions and toward whatever goals he sets for himself. At the same time, it demonstrates where all men are alike, despite diversity of skin color or level of technological development, and reveals in what ways man possesses biosocial characteristics that mark his primate ancestry. Both the facts of human diversity and the points of identity project obvious practical implications of fundamental significance.

Similarly, prehistory and human paleontology, the field of physical anthropology concerned with man's evolutionary past, have together extended man's biological and cultural record in the Old World back well beyond the million-year mark. The almost imperceptibly slow expansion of man's mastery over the physical environment until the last few thousand years is now demonstrated beyond doubt. Moreover, in an increasing number of regions, archaeologists are succeeding in documenting in detail the cultural background of the area, giving a sense of the past and of the accomplishments of earlier ancestral societies. Particularly in developing areas where contemporary societies represent lineal descendants of those of the prehistoric time, the psychological support provided by such knowledge is positive and useful, as these new nations struggle to improve their technological and economic base, westernize, and develop their international posture. Even in areas like the United States, where the dominant population is the result of massive immigration, scientifically sound information about the life of the native groups that existed in past millennia is expanding our awareness in important ways.

To the degree that anthropology provides sound evidence on man's history and on the cultural behavior of all known societies past and present in all corners of the world, it contributes importantly to the liberation of the human mind. It helps us comprehend the world of which we are a part and the events of today which carry us forward into the future.

2
ANTHROPOLOGY AS A BEHAVIORAL AND SOCIAL SCIENCE

Anthropology, as one of the component disciplines of the behavioral and social sciences, has a distinctive history that produces a sense of identity among those who call themselves anthropologists. At the same time, it covers a diverse set of interests overlapping in many ways with its neighboring disciplines, including biological sciences and the humanities. A defining structure is provided by the four commonly recognized subfields: *social-cultural anthropology*, sometimes called ethnology; *archaeology*, to be distinguished from classical archaeology, which tends to be manned by classical scholars; *linguistic anthropology*; and *physical anthropology*. A fifth subfield, less uniformly recognized as a separable component, is *applied anthropology*. The structure of the field as it exists, particularly in the United States, can best be understood by looking at these subfields.

THE FOUR MAJOR SUBFIELDS

The expression *social-cultural anthropology* is used here to indicate the panel's belief that an effort to distinguish sharply between social and cultural anthropology is futile. There are those who would hold to a distinction, with social anthropology limited to interpersonal relations and social groups and cultural anthropology concerned with custom, tradition, and values. However, customs and values involve interpersonal relations, and traditions are passed on through organized social groups. Hence we prefer to treat the two subfields as one, with further internal specializations. More anthropologists acknowledge social-cultural anthropology as their special area of competence than any of the other three major subfields.

Archaeology is the branch of anthropology that involves the excavation and study of the material remains of former cultures. It is the second most populous subfield. Archaeology is really a variety of social-cultural anthropology in its broadest sense, since it is the study of past societies and cultures through their abandoned material remains. Obviously it is easier to find out about some things (such as subsistence techniques) than others (such as language or details of religious ceremonies) through archaeological investigation, but in principle, archaeologists are committed to understanding the implications of their data as fully as possible and some surprisingly detailed and plausible inferences may be made from the information available to them.

There is really no fundamental difference between exploring an Indian mound or an ancient Greek ruin, but as a result of the social history of scholarship the archaeological work of classical antiquity tends to be done by classical scholars, while the study of smaller cultures or the cultures of prehistory is done by anthropologists. These uncertainties as to which discipline belongs where are common to many fields of scholarship; thus when anthropologists study villages on the edge of a large industrial city, or a city ward, or various institutions of the city itself, it is hard to distinguish between their work and that of some sociologists. Increasingly we may expect many of the investigations to become multidisciplinary.

Linguistic anthropology is a branch of the larger field of linguistics, which is concerned with human language in all its aspects. Anthropologists came into this field early because many of the tribes they studied had languages that were little known, and in order to make headway in studying their cultures it was necessary to master the language. A grammar and dictionary of the language were often by-products, but scientific interest went much farther than improving communication with the native users of the language. Languages provide invaluable data for studying the history of peoples; the ways in which languages can differ from one another and the universal features all have in common are of great theoretical interest for the light they shed on the nature of the human mind and of human culture. Linguistic anthropology can be considered a specialized branch of cultural anthropology because language involves customary behavior shared by a community or society. The skills and expertnesses required are such, however, that a specific subfield has developed.

Physical anthropology, essentially a subdivision of human biology, involves the study of the bodily characteristics of men as influenced by heredity and environment. Because of the strong evolutionary interest, much of this research deals with the remains of the most ancient human ancestors, including the anthropoids as man's nearest relatives. However, living and recent populations are also studied, and the behavioral patterns of apes, monkeys, and other primates may be investigated for the light they shed on the biological development of mankind.

This grouping of somewhat disparate subjects under the banner of anthropology is in part a response to a special historical situation: the rapid acculturation and disintegration of many American Indian tribes during the formative period of American anthropology before and after the turn of the century. In their field research the early anthropologists encountered small neglected groups of people, apparently about to lose their identity, who were the last representatives of formerly flourishing native societies. The investigators felt an obligation to science to record all possible information about these vanishing groups: a complete naturalistic description of physique, language, customs, traditions, and even a little of the local archaeology if possible.

INTERRELATIONS AMONG THE SUBFIELDS

The tendency toward specialization commonly leads to the creation of new disciplines. Thus statistics branches off from mathematics and biochemistry separates itself from general chemistry. The different interests of anthropologists with unlike specialities have not resulted in a dismemberment of anthropology, however, because each of the subfields continues to become relevant to the others in newly discovered ways.

There are two major ways in which the data from two or more of the four major subfields are used jointly: (1) in the study of origins of human phenomena, i.e., in tracing the picture of *historical development* from early times to the present and the temporal relations of one human group to another; and (2) in the study of *function* or *process*, i.e., in the study of the operation of culture, of how human groups survive, of the causal relations of various human phenomena interacting within the present or over a relatively short period of time.

Whether in the investigation of historical development or in the study of the functional operation of a culture, anthropologists tend to prefer a "holistic" approach, rather than a piecemeal one. Such an approach—looking at the society and culture in all its aspects as a whole—is obviously facilitated by the choice of small nonliterate societies for study. With such an approach, it is not hard to see why the various anthropological specialties soon come into relation to each other.

In research on the origins of human groups, each of the major subfields of anthropology can provide its own kind of evidence as to the historical relation between two or more groups. Social-cultural anthropology examines oral traditions and attempts to separate fantasy from historical fact. Even more important is the analysis of the comparative content of cultures: how many customs do they have in common? how many beliefs? in what detail? Not all customs are of equal usefulness in the study of ethnic origins. Those customs which are specific adaptations to the geographical environment are not to be expected in a closely related ethnic group living in a different environment. On the other hand, customs that can vary somewhat more freely in relation to the natural environment, such as styles of art or decoration of utensils, religious beliefs and practices, or details of social and political organization, are likely to be especially useful in testing the common origin of two ethnic groups and in measuring the relative distance of their relationship. In archaeology, the main emphasis in testing common origin and measuring separation is on durable artifacts. Where pottery is present the techniques of making and decorating pottery are particularly useful in providing a cultural index, since archaeologists have identified a surprising number of technical variations which characterize precisely the pottery of a culture. Archaeologists also have a variety of ways to date objects—by noting their position in a sequence of deposits or by examining certain kinds of objects for chemical and physical changes that proceed at a measurable rate after manufacture or deposition in an archaeological site.

Linguistic anthropologists are able to identify languages of common origin where they can show that certain words and grammatical processes are shared by two or more languages and where there are regular correspondences between the sounds of two languages in related words. The linguistic anthropologist for the most part studies unwritten languages, so, unlike the linguist dealing with the major Old World languages, he has no old documents to tell him what his language was like centuries earlier. However, by the study of variants in existing languages and by comparing related languages, it is possible to reconstruct the family tree of cognate languages, to distinguish which related words have been in the languages for a long time and which are recent borrowings, and even to reconstruct much of a fairly remote ancestral language.

The physical anthropologist has a variety of methods to measure the biological relationship of two or more human populations, alive or dead. With living populations especially, a number of serological and biochemical tests (such as blood groups and other characteristics of known genetic origin) determine precisely which of a series of known alternant genes an individual possesses and what the frequency of each of these is in the population of which he is a member. In addition to these biochemical tests, physical anthropologists have long used measurements and other direct observations of the human skeleton and other bodily parts to determine how similar two populations are physically and to estimate the amount of common ancestry and the date of their separation.

While any one of the subfields of anthropology can in its own right provide data for inferring the historical connections between ethnic groups, the results are obviously sounder and more convincing if the contributions of more than one subfield can be compared and integrated into a single statement about the ethnic groups under consideration. Collating cultural similarities in surviving recent cultures with the traces of earlier cultures in the archaeological record, relationships between languages, and biological similarities in modern and archaeological populations yields a rather full picture of the development of an ethnic group, at least within recent millennia.

That the four subfields of anthropology can be coordinated in the search for human and ethnic origins does not imply much about possible causal or functional relationships between the objects of study in the different subfields. The search for origins merely assumes that ethnic groups change gradually in all respects—cultural, linguistic, and biological—and that groups that are similar in any of these respects are more closely related than dissimilar groups. Many anthropologists, however, are interested in functional relationships between the subfields of anthropology; some phenomenon in one subfield, say social anthropology, will have some clear connection with something in another subfield, say dialect and style in linguistics. Functional relationships involving all possible pairs of the four subfields of anthropology are under study.

APPLIED ANTHROPOLOGY AS A
FIFTH SUBFIELD

Applied anthropology is best considered a fifth subfield in its own right, although it parallels the four other subfields and possesses elements from each. During the past two decades, a good deal of research has been directed toward using standard anthropological data to solve practical problems. New methods of fact-gathering, a fresh body of data collected with these methods, and the identification of new research areas mark this subfield. Applied physical anthropology is contributing to an understanding of the biological aspects of race, to medicine, and even to the design of specialized clothing and advanced equipment (like supersonic planes and space vehicles) where the limitations and maximum possibilities of the human organism are crucial and must be fully understood. Archaeology is discovering new data about those cultural activities of prehistoric societies that caused fundamental and damaging changes to the physical environment and therefore yield lessons of practical importance for contemporary man. Cultural anthropology is providing technical guidelines to ease the transition of nonindustrial societies under Western influence to a more complex level of socioeconomic organization, of former colonial areas to independent nations, of societies with traditional explanations of disease causation to principles of modern scientific medicine, and so on. Applied cultural anthropology is likewise developing procedures by which action programs of international and governmental agencies (e.g., UNESCO and the Peace Corps) may be evaluated in terms of basic design and their success in attaining announced objectives. Linguistic anthropology is producing the language information, technical and practical, that is necessary to encourage the advance of literacy in societies with unwritten languages.

Applied anthropology, if carefully fostered and kept tightly scientific in methodology, offers great promise to those anthropologists who elect to make a professional commitment to improving man's lot. At the same time, the potential for a rich backflow of raw data to the more strictly scientific aspects of the discipline cannot be overlooked. Hypotheses drawn from "pure" data are ordinarily difficult to examine experimentally, but they may sometimes be tested in the field under nearly experimental conditions by anthropologists in a position to observe the effects on societies of administrative action with specific, practical objectives in mind. This field of anthropology is certain to receive increased research emphasis during the coming decades until, it may be predicted, it becomes a unit of major dimensions within the discipline.

The preceding paragraph suggests a revealing contrast between applied anthropology and other applied fields. In general, the "practitioners" of a field, those who apply its findings to practical problems, contribute little to the growth of the knowledge of that field. Distinctions like those between physician and medical researcher, politician and political scientist, and social worker and sociologist come readily to mind. The facts noted above reveal, however, that the applied anthropologist fails to fit in a parallel dyad against the cultural and other anthropologists. He does not need to lose his role as an anthropological scientist in order to be able to serve the needs of a developing society.

RELATIONSHIPS BETWEEN ANTHROPOLOGY
AND OTHER BEHAVIORAL SCIENCES ..

Up to this point we have considered the subdivisions of anthropology and their interrelationships. It is now appropriate to consider the relations between anthropology and various related disciplines, including the other social and behavioral sciences, the humanities, the biological sciences, and the physical sciences.

In colleges and universities anthropology has often been grouped in a single department with sociology or in a general department of social sciences including perhaps economics, political science, and psychology as well. There is obviously much in common between social anthropology and sociology: both are concerned with explaining how societies work and how they keep going. In practice, there has tended to be a working division in which sociologists study large modern societies, especially their own, and anthropologists study small underdeveloped societies, especially remote foreign ones. However, a majority of practitioners of both disciplines would probably deny these limitations on their data. Many anthropologists have worked in large modern societies, at any rate, and the proportion doing so is likely to increase. We may doubt whether it is possible to produce a generally accepted definition of the two disciplines that would separate them unequivocally in all cases, nor is it perhaps desirable to do so. However, we may cite several differences in emphasis that, when taken together, will differentiate the majority of social anthropologists from the majority of sociologists. One important difference is in methodological emphasis: the sociologist typically engages in the extensive, large-scale study of some rather precise questions; he is greatly concerned about the adequacy of his sample of subjects or respondents, or the accuracy of the data of others which he uses in secondary analysis. In contrast, the anthropologist typically conducts a more intensive clinical study of individuals as exemplars of sociocultural process; he is interested in many questions and he is willing to large extent to let his subjects or "informants" (a good word in anthropology, not the same at all as "informers" in politics) decide what they want to talk about; he is more concerned with establishing an intimate relationship with a few people who will talk with him freely and frankly than with selecting a representative sample. Both types of study obviously have their uses: work with informants produces much rich information, but some check is desirable to know how representative it is.

Social anthropology also has a substantial overlap of interest with economics, considered as the study of the production and distribution of goods. While not all societies have a fully developed monetary economy, all societies do have scarce goods and some means of exchange. Anthropologists are interested in exploring the range of production and distribution systems in human societies and in understanding the particular system in the society being studied at a given time. Most anthropologists are not scientifically interested in the operation of the economy of our own society; the typical non-anthropological economist, on the other hand, is extremely interested in the operation of our own economy. He will not ordinarily show much interest in the operation of greatly different economic systems.

Social anthropology has another substantial overlap of interest with political science. In contrast to the dominant trend in sociology, political scientists, like anthropologists, are interested in relationships between societies, both international relations and interethnic relations within nations. If the economy—the production and distribution of goods—is one tie that holds all societies together, the political system—the system of control of the legitimate use of force—is another major tie. No social system can be understood without the investigation of both of these major ties. The interests of social anthropologists contrast with those of political scientists, even when they study the same societies. The social anthropologist usually does not restrict himself as closely as the political scientist to the local political system. Moreover, the work of the political scientist in foreign areas often is concerned mainly with problems of modernization policy: how fast and to what extent can modern democratic practices be introduced into the area? The anthropologist is likely to have less of a commitment to find how the society might be changed and is inclined instead to wonder simply how the political system works and what its ties are with the past. If the system does change, will it become more or less like ours?

Social anthropology and linguistic anthropology both have overlapping interests with parts of psychology, itself a very diverse discipline. Social-cultural anthropologists, in their work with informants, have obvious close ties with clinical psychology and psychiatry. Both are trying to understand individuals in detail and in depth, although the anthropologist is studying the individual as an exemplar of his culture, while the psychiatrist or clinical psychologist usually takes the culture for granted and tries to understand the deviations that single an individual out from other participants in his culture. Ideally, the anthropologist ought to know enough about clinical psychology to be able to distinguish the idiosyncratic components in his data from the cultural. In fact, practitioners of both disciplines probably tend to make the expected errors of interpretation from time to time: a clinical psychologist is likely at times to interpret some standard belief or practice of a client from a different ethnic group as an individual neurotic symptom, while an anthropologist is likely at times to exaggerate the cultural significance of some individual aberrations.

A final social science which has an important degree of overlap with social-cultural anthropology is geography. Geographers share with anthropologists the tendency to specialize in a particular part of the world. Geographers, like cultural anthropologists, are interested in the use men make of their physical and natural environment and the modifications they bring about in it. However, geographers are typically more focused on the items of culture with which they are mainly concerned. Geographers are primarily concerned with human activities and objects that modify the natural environment or involve some transaction with it: farming, mining, architecture and city planning, highways, waterways, railways. The interests of the cultural anthropologist overlap, but are somewhat broader, for he is also interested in aspects of culture not very closely conditioned by the environment, such as language, literature and the arts, religion.

RELATIONSHIPS BETWEEN ANTHROPOLOGY
AND OTHER FIELDS OF SCHOLARSHIP

There is little point in making up a catalog of all the interrelationships between anthropology and fields of scholarship outside the behavioral and social sciences, except to point to a few areas in which the affiliations have been particularly close.

A number of areas bring anthropologists and humanists together, such as the study of art, music, and religion. A particularly noteworthy field is that of folklore. The folklorist of modern society is interested in the anonymous oral literature and art of recent culture. The discipline of folklore in the United States has been a union between humanists who moved into the area from the study of literature and cultural-social anthropologists who moved into it from the study of the traditional oral literature of primitive societies.

Many of the linguistics departments springing up in our universities have come into being through a union of linguistic anthropologists with classical linguists and other language specialists, often from the foreign language departments of the universities moving in this direction. Their common interests require no documentation.

Prehistory and recorded history merge into each other, so that the archaeological anthropologist's interest in prehistory merges with the classical archaeologist's interest in civilizations with a recorded history and with the historian's interest in understanding the march of events. Anthropology, under the influence of the concept of evolution, is the most historical-minded discipline within the social sciences, outside history itself, and in its time perspective exceeds our usual conception of history.

Physical anthropology is very closely related to other sciences of human biology, particularly anatomy, genetics, and evolution, but the interest merges also with comparative psychology (particularly in the evolution of behavior and the social behavior of animal aggregates). Some anthropologists work in medical schools, in which the social-cultural interests may be as relevant as the biological ones.

These few paragraphs merely hint at the many interrelationships. Modern science requires specialization because of the complex skills required of the scientist. At the same time, the specialist must be ready to "look aside," and to draw, through collaborative effort, on the expertness of many others besides himself—often those from disciplines other than his own. Because of its interest in all aspects of the societies it studies, anthropology, perhaps more than other sciences, needs to keep itself open to all available information.

3
SOCIAL AND CULTURAL ANTHROPOLOGY

The major subfields of anthropology, as previously noted, have sufficiently disparate characteristics so that their methods and substance require somewhat further specification if anthropology as it exists today is to be better understood. In this and the three following chapters each of the major subfields will be considered in turn: social-cultural anthropology in this chapter, followed by archaeology, linguistic anthropology, and physical anthropology in the succeeding ones.

HISTORICAL BACKGROUND OF CONTEMPORARY SOCIAL-CULTURAL ANTHROPOLOGY

In the United States social and cultural anthropology are often interchangeable terms for the study of man as a social being with a cultural heritage. Some anthropologists emphasize social relationships and their regulation; others concentrate upon intellectual and emotional creativity. Whatever the particular emphasis, all base their work upon the concept of "culture," the basic theoretical discovery of nineteenth-century anthropology, which has long since been absorbed into the intellectual kit of the social and behavioral sciences. It was a matter of common experience that human behavior is highly variable from one social group to the next and that patterns of behavior change over time. Edward Tylor had the wit to realize

31

that this common experience pointed to a phenomenon that could be studied in its own right. Writing a hundred years ago (in 1865), he called it "culture"; we also owe the word "anthropology" to him. Anthropologists set out to chart the dimensions of culture with the hope that eventually they would discover the conditions that influenced cultural developments.

Before the twentieth century was far advanced, they had evidence that much that had once been regarded as natural behavior was in fact highly specific to particular groups and was learned by the members of these groups as part of their cultural heritage. This applied to such apparently natural facilities as ways of hearing, seeing, standing, and breathing. It applied even more to social codes, including systems of value. These were matters of custom taught by one generation to the next. A child was born with the ability to learn the cultural code presented to him rather than with a set towards one particular code. No evidence has appeared to challenge the primacy of culture as an explanation for the differences in behavior that distinguish social groups from one another. The discovery has had an enormous impact upon contemporary life, comparable to the effect of the basic discoveries in physical science. We are still learning to live with our new knowledge.

For decades anthropological research was directed towards discovering the whole range of culture, a goal that involved the examination of the cultural life of every group of men. Anthropologists therefore stressed research on little-known or newly discovered peoples. Recording new cultural variants replaced anthropology's earlier concern with the way in which culture had evolved over the history of mankind. The greatest prizes went to those who could report strikingly new variants and much less attention was given to the implications of the uniformities that were also being discovered. In the extreme form, some anthropology became a mere catalog of strange customs. Nevertheless, as anthropologists talked with men who had little technical equipment and whose way of life appeared to be a jumble of odd belief and practice, anthropologists were learning that they were faced with intelligent men and women whose lives had meaning and integrity. It became an anthropological principle that each society or cultural system should be examined as a valid solution to the problems of existence faced by all men. No one solution was the yardstick by which the worth of the others could be measured. Anthropologists in the 1920s and 1930s may have been somewhat naive in their acceptance of this principle of "cultural relativism," but it allowed them to step outside themselves and ask what a particular way of life meant to those who practiced it. Any cultural item had its meaning in relation to the overall system within which it was found.

Anthropologists had begun to think in terms of social and cultural systems rather than in terms of disparate, unrelated conglomerates of customs, brought together by historical accident, that could be changed at will. They were prepared for the possibility of examining the impact of particular changes over a wide field of social life. They learned to ask themselves how economic activities, family organization, legal and political codes, mythology, ritual, and artistic styles might be interconnected and mutually interdependent. Probably no anthropologist today would argue that any people have ever had a completely integrated culture, any more than they have had one that was completely static. They use the idea of integration as a working assumption that permits them to ask about particular interconnections and the likelihood that one change may invoke a series of other changes. It has not been easy to move from this point to more rigorous methods for testing hypotheses about significant relationships. Anthropology is concerned with a whole complex of behavior with which it deals in a comparative fashion. Before the development of sophisticated methods of data analysis, anthropologists could rarely apply tests for the validity of any set of hypotheses. Even now they are only on the threshold of being able to measure any very complex cultural phenomena.

Nevertheless, the period before World War II produced a number of contributions to anthropological theory and to social thought in general that are still significant. Anthropologists of that period began to test the applicability outside Western societies of generalizations proposed by other social sciences. Margaret Mead was perhaps most influential in establishing the principle that field work in non-Western societies provided the equivalent of a laboratory for the testing of social hypotheses. On the basis of her work in Oceania she challenged current beliefs about the nature of masculine and feminine personality traits and showed that these changed from society to society and were not due solely to biological considerations. Her work on adolescence in Samoa showed a link between adolescent stress and particular kinds of social arrangements.

In the same period Bronislaw Malinowski in Melanesia and E. E. Evans-Pritchard in Africa were doing equally challenging work in their attack upon the notion that there was such a thing as "primitive mentality." They showed that, given their premises, Melanesians and Africans behaved as rationally as Europeans and Americans. They were intelligent men and women, operating at the same level of adult responsibility as their age-mates in other societies, and had comprehensible reasons for what they did. They could not be taken to represent earlier stages of psychological development through which Western man had passed, nor were they to be compared to children in Western society. Their beliefs were shown to comprise logical systems, using the same techniques of inference as Western logic. It was not necessary to invent a new psychology or a new philosophy to understand their point of view.

Simultaneously, social-anthropological field research methods underwent a great change in the United States, following in large measure the earlier developments in Britain. Prior to the war relatively few American anthropologists made extended field trips; more often they followed the pattern set by Franz Boas, A. L. Kroeber, and R. H. Lowie of the shorter trip, perhaps a summer vacation, coupled with intensive interviewing of a few "key" informants. After the war, field research money became available on an unprecedented scale, and the year-long intensive study of a single community became the rule rather than the exception. Participant observation, including learning the local language, replaced informants and translators. For the first time in the United States, data became sufficiently plentiful to permit the anthropologist to generalize from his own field materials, rather than, as previously, being forced to accept the informant's statement that "that's how we do it." Much more than formerly, the anthropologist could approach a description of a "real" culture, rather than having to be content with an "ideal" culture as described by a handful of informants. Important conceptual developments also accompanied this change in field method. First, anthropological interests became increasingly sociological, concerned with the structure and function of social systems rather than with the exhaustive cataloging of all phases of a single culture. And second, concern with origins and past history began to take second place to interest in the dynamic processes of culture change.

Some anthropologists, of course, have continued to be interested in the reconstruction of the unwritten history of primitive peoples and with the development of civilizations. But in a rapidly changing world, with rural-to-urban migrations going on before our eyes, with the diffusion of city ways to villages, with more changes in attitudes, beliefs, and customs in a decade than formerly occurred in a thousand years, it is not surprising that a majority of anthropologists have come to concentrate on these processes of modernization, on cultural dynamics, and on the causes and consequences of change.

The old theoretical models, which assumed that cultures were integrated wholes, became inadequate to deal with situations of rapid change and the complex interrelationships between rural and urban areas and between local and national or international events. The assumption that cultures were moral systems became difficult to use when practitioners of a way of life no longer regarded it with favor. When the people of a society held many different beliefs, it became difficult to see belief systems as logical systems. The way was open to younger anthropologists to repudiate old models that emphasized cultural integration, stable systems, and the significance of traditional values. They attempted to develop analytical models emphasizing processes of change, flexibility of choice, and the necessity for decisions.

The impact of World War II and the events of the immediately succeeding period also forced anthropologists to examine the implications of "cultural relativism." They found they could not avoid making judgments about forms of behavior when they themselves were intimately affected by the consequences of that behavior. Since then there has been a growing concern to find some basis for making judgments that would depend on universal criteria rather than on the value systems of one particular culture. It is therefore no accident that anthropologists at the same time began to turn away from concern with the range of cultural variability, towards which so much of early research had been pressed. Increasingly they have been trying to define universal qualities characteristic of all cultures, which involves them in a search for the organizing principles behind the mass of specific cultural features. This has also brought social and cultural anthropologists back into closer association with physical anthropologists, who have continued their research into the biological nature of man. It has also once more become legitimate to build schemes of social and cultural evolution and to seek to link current ways of life to their origins in the remote past. If much of early twentieth-century research went to show how culture conditioned biological responses, much of recent work has looked to the underlying biological processes that determine the nature of social responses.

By the 1950s anthropology had made major contributions to social thought—the concept of culture, the mapping of major dimensions of cultural variability, the development of analytic methods associated with functional systems, a demonstration of the psychic unity of mankind, and a body of field techniques for the study of cultural systems, including the microstudy. They had also developed a technical vocabulary for descriptive work across cultural frontiers. They had realized the necessity for a professional ethic that respected the rights of the subjects of their research.

THE EVOLVING METHODS
OF SOCIAL-CULTURAL ANTHROPOLOGY

About a hundred years ago, anthropologists began to take responsibility for collecting as well as analyzing data on other societies. This did not lead to a rapid increase in information since opportunities for professional employment were few and funds for field work meager. The production of reliable new information was expectably small. Until approximately 1950, established professionals could keep abreast of reports incorporating new field data. They expected to read the reports based on different geographical regions and emphasizing quite different aspects of social life. This was of considerable importance because anthropologists usually develop their theoretical ideas as a commentary on particular sets of field data rather than on abstract formulations.

Data Banks

As early as the 1930s, George Murdock and others interested in comparative work began to experiment with data banks of one kind or another. One developed into the still useful Human Relations Area Files, which abstracts and classifies data from a selected sample of cultures, using a classification system that reflects earlier interests in the subject. It does not seek to cope with the great mass of incoming data and its format does not adapt easily to new research interests. So far no form of data bank has been developed that can serve satisfactorily the present needs of anthropology. This is an area where there is urgent need for imaginative experimentation.

Kinship Studies

In early field studies almost any kind of data proved useful, but as the science of anthropology advances data are studied in relation to some kind of conceptual pattern or theory. Contemporary anthropologists see man as an ordering animal, who needs to construct a knowable world out of the flux of experience with which he is faced. The problem for the anthropologist is to find out how men derive the categories with which they work and to discover the common ordering principles. This emphasis can be found in the writings of Claude Levi-Strauss, the French anthropologist who is one of the vital intellectual figures of the contemporary world. One rigorous method for studying principles of classification over a broad array of cultures uses formal analysis of kinship terminology. The American anthropologists Alfred Kroeber and Robert Lowie gave one answer to the problem of order when they showed that eight principles could account for all variations of kinship terminology so far known to us.

Kinship terminologies, along with other ethno-science data, can be used as an experimental ground for testing the possible relevance of precise quantitative models for anthropological work. They therefore loom large at the moment.

Statistics and Mathematical Models

Anthropologists interested in change are turning to the use of statistical techniques and are experimenting with mathematical models of one kind or another. This practice arises partly from the scale of the societies with which they now work, where sampling may be necessary and quantitative data are available. Clifford Geertz, in examining the failure of Indonesia to reach a point of economic takeoff, based much of his argument on the available statistics for population growth, agricultural production, export figures, and so forth. The new interest in statistics and mathematical models also arises from the fact that many anthropologists now seek to deal with events that can be counted rather than with ideal patterns of behavior. Frederik Barth has experimented with game theory as a model for handling the formation of political alliances among Swat Pathans, the participation of farmers in working parties among the Fur of the Sudan, and the choice of fishing strategies by captains and crews in the Norwegian fishing fleet. The assumption that men have a choice among a number of alternatives in even the most traditional of societies emphasizes the need to examine the consequences of such choices for the continuity of institutions.

Much of the work now being done by those who call themselves social anthropologists develops from interests similar to those of Barth. Social anthropologists ask how people respond to conflicting possibilities, how the choices they make affect future choices, and how these in turn redefine the situations in which men find themselves. Their method is adapted to the study of political life in a period of rapid change when rules change in the process of being enacted and men change their roles as they learn them. It assumes no long-term stability of structure nor any deep-seated commitment to existing social institutions. The method is also useful in studies of urban life during a period when more and more men move into the cities and city institutions cannot absorb the host of newcomers.

THE FUTURE OF SOCIAL-CULTURAL ANTHROPOLOGY

The early interest in reconstructing the culture of isolated groups of people through a study of their oral literature and interpersonal behavior can survive only a few years longer, as modern travel and communication destroy the isolation of peoples. Many problems of comparative culture will persist, of course, and work with the older objectives can continue, but in somewhat altered form.

The disappearance of isolated societies does not, however, foreshadow a decreasing interest in social and cultural anthropology. On the contrary, as the foregoing discussion has indicated, anthropologists have become increasingly interested in the problems of contemporary society, including the larger-sized industrial societies, and their methods are applicable to institutions and subgroups within these cultures as well as to the more isolated or primitive ones. Furthermore, the social changes when originally more isolated cultures come into close contact with more advanced, industrialized groups raise many new and important problems.

Far from being a field of declining interest because of the disappearance of field opportunities, anthropology sees the problems on the horizon as of ever-increasing scope. Anthropology is a field where many more trained workers are needed.

4
ARCHAEOLOGY

A primary concern of anthropology has always been the study of cultural development. Thus, archaeology—the reconstruction of past cultures and the processes at work on them—has always been an important aspect of anthropological research. Archaeological remains constitute the only surviving record from the 99 per cent of human cultural development that preceded the invention of writing. It is precisely these remains, suggestive of man's first steps along and parallel to the road to civilization, that have given meaning and focus to the whole study of human cultural development.

Anthropologists do not, of course, have a monopoly on the practice of archaeology. Historians, philologists, art historians, and simple collectors of *objets d'art* all have an interest in the remains of the past, and all have engaged fairly systematically in archaeological excavations at one time or another. Yet as a general rule, the systematic investigation of the prehistoric past has been largely the province of anthropologists, while remains of more recent eras have fallen chiefly to the philologist and the collector, who was often interested in the things to be recovered, such as coins or statues, rather than in their theoretical significance.

For many and obvious reasons—not the least, financial—the principal focus of American archaeology has always been upon America's own aboriginal past. As a result, the cultural history of the American Indian is known in surprising detail over a very large part of the two continents, despite the fact that he has left us no intelligible written records. The picture of aboriginal cultural development in the Americas over ten millennia, painstakingly reconstructed from thousands of sites and their artifactual content, constitutes the outstanding and indeed unique achievement of American archaeology to date.

At the same time, many American archaeologists have retained an active interest in the cultures of the Old World, which are more nearly a part of their own historical background, and in recent years the availability of research funds has enabled a few of them to translate this interest into practical excavations. The meticulous techniques of excavation and analysis that were developed in the study of New World prehistory have proven equally valuable in the Old, and have enabled Americans to play a leading part in the investigation of early civilization in the Near East, the Mediterranean basin, and North Africa.

Thus, American archaeology finds itself today in a period of rapidly expanding horizons. While its primary concern for American Indian prehistory continues unabated, the study is losing much of its early provincialism and is beginning to take its place in a worldwide, multidisciplinary synthesis of knowledge and theory about human cultural development.

ORIENTATIONS OF AMERICAN ARCHAEOLOGISTS

Archaeology as practiced by North American anthropologists can be viewed historically by describing the development of three separate orientations Americans have used to view the prehistoric past. They are here called the speculative, the descriptive-historic, and the problem-related. While these ways of looking at the past arose in sequence, all three continue in the present, at various levels of popularity, to direct the main activities and interests of certain archaeologists, whether professional or amateur.

The Speculative Orientation

Soon after the discovery of North America, it was realized that not only were there aborigines but also that the continent was the site of remains of inhabitants not represented by the living groups. These remains precipitated interest in what would now be called genuine archaeological questions: how old are they, who made them, what were they used for, how do they relate to the living aborigines, and so forth. And these questions in turn prompted further observation and speculation. However, this early data collection was unorganized and uncritical, and there was no systematic means of communication between those few untrained individuals who had more than a casual interest in these developing problems.

The major results of the speculations prior to 1850 included the assumptions that the prehistoric remains: (1) were relatively recent; (2) were not related to the contemporary Indian aborigines; (3) represented a "higher" way of life than that of the historic Indian; (4) were homogeneous and represented only one culture; and (5) were left by such groups as the Welsh, lost tribes of Israel, Egyptians, Phoenicians, or occupants of the lost continents of Atlantis or Mu. It is interesting to note that a large part of the general public still views prehistoric remains in North America in terms of these same explanatory elements.

The Descriptive-Historic Orientation

Near the middle of the nineteenth century a new orientation began to direct archaeological interests. Beginning slowly and making little impression at first, it gradually became the major focus of professional archaeology. This descriptive-historic orientation emphasizes the controlled observation, collection, and classification of data and their placement in time. This stage was the beginning of archaeology with a purpose and it involved all the traditional elements of the natural history stage of science.

Although it is difficult to trace the precise factors affecting the development of this period, it is undoubtedly due in part to the double influence of the growth of science and philosophical rationalism in the nineteenth century. In anthropology this movement is best reflected in the contemporary empiricism of Boas and his students.

For the first time American archaeology practiced organized observation and collection of information through survey and excavation. Much of the artifactual data was to be deposited in museums, which in many cases initially dispatched the collecting expeditions. By 1900, academically trained archaeologists began to appear and to accelerate this change in the nature of the discipline, and in the 1930s large-scale excavations with the assistance of federal relief labor climaxed these efforts. As the data accumulated, the need for organization grew and classification systems proliferated. With a developing awareness of time-depth, these systems gradually developed from strictly geographical groupings with no chronological scale to complicated systems that incorporated time, space, and form, and often became an end in themselves. The systematic communication necessary for the growing science was provided by organized publication, initially through government outlets and later through professional journals.

When the results of this intensified, organized activity began to appear in print, the basis for the earlier speculations dissolved. Gradually the concept that the past occupants were not Indian became unpopular and was replaced by the assumption of aboriginal continuity. The pendulum then swung in the opposite direction and it became fashionable to attribute all prehistoric remains to the ethnic group that had historically occupied, if not the immediate area, at least one in the close vicinity. This direct historic assumption itself changed to the direct historic approach, which merely attempted to work from the present to the past in order to obtain a clearer view of prehistory. Finally, the availability of increased time-depth and the growing awareness of cultural heterogeneity fostered an interest in discovering the development of the cultural sequences locally, regionally, and continentally.

Virtually all amateur archaeologists continue today to operate from the descriptive-historic orientation, as do most professional archaeologists. They continue to search for better excavation and recording techniques and are deeply concerned with problems of description, classification, and chronological placement. The fact that important advances are still being made in this area is evident, since it was not until 1950 that the radiocarbon dating technique was developed to provide the first sound temporal framework for most of North American prehistory.

The Problem-Related Orientation

Just prior to World War II a change became apparent in cultural anthropology generally, reflected in a growing concern for something beyond the pure description of primitive tribes, which previously had been the mainstay of anthropology; a questioning of the potentiality for human beings to develop an endless variety of cultures; a renewed search for cultural universals and the limitations set by man's physical constitution and his environment; and more concern for problem-solving. As early as 1935, A. L. Kroeber, recognizing the developing conflict between these new interests and the more traditional descriptive orientation of anthropology, wrote, "The two need not conflict. . . . The scientific element has freed anthropology from some of the limitations of conventional history."

These same changes toward a more scientific, generalizing approach were soon reflected in North American archaeology. They first appeared in general articles emphasizing the need for functional studies and a broader participation by archaeologists in the conceptual and theoretical developments of general anthropology. Somewhat later attempts at implementation were made, as represented by studies more concerned with process, evolutionary concepts, and comparative generalizations. In addition, more American archaeologists were beginning to work on sites and on problems in the Old World. The beginnings of agriculture, the origins of urban life and civilization, and similar problems were examined with the help of field techniques first developed on the remains of the American Indian. While today the number of such studies is miniscule and the group of archaeologists producing work with a true cross-cultural orientation is even smaller, there are indications that both will grow. The new emphasis can be seen in newly stated goals of archaeology: (1) to seek regularities that enable a clearer understanding of human behavior anywhere at any time; and (2) to discover regularities that are in a sense spaceless and timeless.

THEORY IN ARCHAEOLOGY

Archaeology has developed no separate body of primary theories. Its theoretical postulates are those of cultural anthropology

—with the concept of culture being of prime importance. The basic assumption of most archaeological research, then, is that the behavior of a group tends not to be random, but rather that the individuals who constitute it conform to a series of cultural patterns. Therefore, one of the first tasks of the archaeologist is to discover those patterns that interrelate to form the total culture of the group being studied. It is basically this approach that comprises one of the three theoretical models currently in use in American archaeology. The three can be called: (1) the functional or conjunctive model, (2) the historical model, and (3) the evolutionary model. The first model, seeking to find the patterns that interrelate the characteristics of a given culture, is a sophisticated outgrowth of the earlier descriptive orientation. The approach stresses the reconstruction of as much of the culture as possible, as well as the interrelationships of its parts.

The second theoretical model currently used in archaeology emphasizes a strictly historical theoretical structure, stressing the search for local, regional, and continental culture histories. It assumes that each of these is historically unique, yet it is as a result of work done from this perspective that archaeology has been able to present to the modern world the main outlines of its rise from the primitive condition. It has been able to trace the growth of civilizations on three continents, while unveiling some of man's greatest works of art and architecture.

The third theoretical position, popular among contemporary archaeologists, is the evolutionary. Julian Steward's presentation of multilinear evolution has given an important impetus to this approach to archaeology. It has allowed the archaeologist to utilize and work toward regional sequences of cultural development, while at the same time encouraging problem-directed interests oriented toward general problems of broad cultural development.

This interest has prompted archaeologists not only to chronicle the rise of civilizations in the Near East, Asia, and the New World, but also to ask whether these possess similar lines of growth and patterns of development. There is every indication that this theoretical model will provide the cross-culturally historical questions that will elicit from archaeology those contributions most meaningful to the theoretical development of anthropology.

Archaeology has provided the data for testing a great variety of hypotheses in the realm of cultural development and change, which are among anthropology's major concerns. It has provided an essential check on theories of cultural evolution and is substituting fact for fancy in such matters as the origins of plant and animal domestication and the beginnings of writing, urbanization, and other crucial steps toward civilization.

ARCHAEOLOGICAL TECHNIQUES

Four general technical stages characterize the recovery of archaeological data: survey, test excavation, major excavation, and analysis. The basic technique of archaeological survey is the systematic examination of an area, searching for the cultural or physical remains that suggest evidence of human occupation. Recently new and refined techniques, including aerial reconnaissance, electrical prospection, and refined sampling theory, have been added to the archaeologist's bag of tools and the number of such new techniques will undoubtedly increase.

Once sites are located, it may be necessary to determine something of their contents. This is usually accomplished by the collection of cultural material from the surface for later examination in the laboratory or by use of such newly developed techniques as testing for differences in magnetism or electrical resistivity below the surface, which may be caused by residues of cultural activities. A small exploratory test of the site is frequently made to increase the probability of recovering what is expected, since no site should be excavated unless it is fairly certain that new information will result from the work.

Excavation techniques vary with the conditions of the site and the problem orientation of the archaeologist. While long-handled shovels, picks, and trowels are the most commonly used equipment, bulldozers, roadgraders, and backhoes are often helpful to clear sterile overburden from deeply buried sites or from sites that must be excavated quickly because of impending destruction. Some sites, on the other hand, are dug with tools no larger than knives, brushes, and dental picks.

The analysis of excavated material is based initially upon its classification into workable categories and upon a description of the criteria used in establishing these categories and of the artifacts placed within them. At first, classification of cultural material is based on visual observation of form and material, but technical analyses by metallurgists, chemists, physicists, geologists, and biologists are now being used much more frequently not only in the classification but also in interpretation of data.

To be of historical importance the reconstructed cultures which are the result of archaeological analysis must be put into a chronological framework. A great deal of effort has gone into the development of techniques of dating, yet only in recent years have really important advances been made in this area. The work of outside specialists has become extremely important in providing such techniques as radiocarbon dating, thermoluminescent and magnetic dating, and obsidian hydration, as well as older standbys like dating by geological strata or tree-rings.

Since each scrap of recoverable material may be of significance in solving the problem at hand, archaeologists save vast amounts of data from each site. For this reason, archaeological data lend themselves well to statistical treatment. The use of computers in archaeological analysis will certainly become increasingly important as their potential is more fully understood and their programming becomes more generally a part of the graduate curriculum.

Archaeological work has thus far been concentrated in North and Middle America, Europe, and the Near East, with some rewarding results. With new techniques and approaches to interpretation, these areas will profitably continue to be centers of archaeological activity. However, the remainder of the world is not nearly so well known archaeologically, and, although there are pockets of knowledge about prehistory (as for example, in parts of Southeast Asia, Japan, Russia, Peru, and Oceania), the prehistory of most of the rest of the world is largely unknown in any detail. Thus in terms of any overall knowledge of the total pattern and sequence of human prehistory, archaeologists have only begun. In a sense those areas that have been well worked are serving as a testing ground for new ideas and approaches so that the pioneer areas may profit by the accumulation of knowledge, techniques, and conceptualization.

CONSERVATION OF ARCHAEOLOGICAL SITES

The basic data of archaeology come from the accumulated remains of prehistoric usage: village sites, religious monuments, trash heaps, and so forth. But unlike the social anthropologist, whose data are constantly available from the activities of living men, or the linguistic anthropologist, who has a steady source of information in the contemporary speech, the archaeologist has available only a limited amount of data. The basic material of archaeology is rapidly being destroyed by urban expansion, highway construction, land leveling, flood control, and the activities of amateur "relic" collectors. Archaeologists and government officials have long recognized this problem and have sought to cope with it through the development of conservation programs. The extensive archaeological salvage operations in flood-control reservoirs are an outstanding example of such an effort. Although this program could stand improvement, it does at least represent a tremendous investment of federal funds for the recovery of some of the remains of American prehistoric heritage. The federal government has even contributed to the salvage of archaeological material in other countries, such as those in Egypt and Nubia.

But since there is a finite amount of prehistoric archaeological data and because it can never be replaced once it has been destroyed, a much more comprehensive approach to the problem of archaeological conservation is needed. Two such approaches are suggested here. First, the federal and state agencies that already contribute to the salvage of archaeological remains need more positive coordination. Furthermore, those federal agencies and private organizations whose activities destroy archaeological material should develop an overall policy to insure its protection. The Committee on the Recovery of Archaeological Remains, which has done a magnificent job in initiating and directing this kind of work in the past, needs more government support and encouragement.

Antiquity laws also need to be strengthened on the local, state, and federal levels as a positive step toward the preservation of the archaeological resources of the United States. A great deal of the destruction comes from the senseless looting of archaeological sites by amateur archaeologists and relic collectors. The same kind of recognition must be given to the vanishing archaeological resources as is given to other natural resources, such as migratory birds, that are threatened by annihilation. Other countries far less developed than the United States have much more rigid antiquities laws protecting their archaeological remains, a clear recognition of the importance they place on them. These laws need to be studied and considered as possible approaches to the protection of similar materials in this country before this irreplaceable resource completely disappears.

ARE THERE PRACTICAL CONSEQUENCES FLOWING FROM ARCHAEOLOGICAL RESEARCH?

Of the four traditional areas of anthropology, archaeology has to the present demonstrated the fewest practical applications. Indeed, few archaeologists have explicitly expressed interest in exploring the potential practical applications of their field. Like history, archaeology in its studies of past civilizations fails to possess commanding relevance to the contemporary problems of man. At the most general level, of course, relevance exists. The proposition that the past must be known and its lessons comprehended if the errors of history are not to be repeated is as applicable to archaeology as to recorded history. Despite a concentration in archaeology on "pure" science, however, some specific insights upon issues of importance today can be observed.

First, archaeology, through its findings, provides basic data used in other fields with some elements of practical interest in mind. It is the archaeologist, for example, who uncovers and dates the human skeletal material analyzed by the paleopathologist and by the physical anthropologist concerned with the long history of human disease.

In exploiting his physical and biological surroundings, man has in large measure and over much of the world remade his environment. How this has come about is revealed by some of the studies made by archaeologists. In the view of G. W. Dimbleby, for example, forests would now be thriving in parts of the British Isles where hill-peat presently grows "if there had not been repeated destruction by fire and grazing from Mesolithic times onwards."

A second illustration exemplifies the use of archaeology in interpreting climatological phenomena. Following careful field observations and applying sound meteorological theory, Reid A. Bryson, in company with other meteorologists, hypothesized that the great Indian desert of Rajputana should in fact be no more than a semiarid region. The air above contains far more moisture than normal over desert areas. The meteorologists attributed the unusual aridity to the enormous quantities of dust constantly suspended above this desert. The questions then became: How can the presence of this dust be explained? Has it always existed? Is the desert in any sense man-made? Here archaeology entered. Archaeologists have demonstrated that until about 1500 B.C. this area of northwestern India and eastern West Pakistan was occupied by farmers who raised cows and pigs and practiced extensive grain cultivation. About 1500 B.C., however, this civilization of Harappa and Mohenjo-Daro vanished. What was the sequence of events which led to this calamity? Bryson and David A. Baerreis, his archaeological colleague, speculated that, when these prehistoric cultivators entered the region, it was an area of grassland, as the present moisture content of the air mass over the region would permit. As the population increased, the natural vegetation was progressively stripped in field construction. Gradually the surface area from which the winds could gather dust grew. As the dust content of the air increased, a drying effect resulted, following well-established meteorological principles. The system became self-perpetuating: as the average yield per unit dropped, more and more areas were denuded to create fields. About 1500 B.C., the breaking-point in the spiraling system was reached and the civilization, no longer able to support its population, collapsed, killed by the dust of its own creating. The practical implications are manifest: since man and his past cultural behavior are evidently responsible for the Rajputana Desert, carefully controlled land utilization practices should permit the native grasses to again seed and mature. With the soil stabilized, precipitation should increase and the earlier richer environment should return, with greatly increased productivity. A practical course of action for Indian agronomists is suggested.

Finally, the possibilities of using to practical advantage knowledge attained by earlier civilizations and discovered by us through archaeological research are illustrated by recent experiments in the Negev Desert. Archaeologists have revealed the remarkable extent to which the desert dwellers of two millennia ago were able to till these arid sands by constructing catchment basins and excavating cisterns beneath dry washes. Putting this information to practical use and employing the same basins, Professor Evanari of Hebrew University is now raising crops in the middle of this arid region. Moreover, he hopes not only to utilize similar ancient irrigation systems elsewhere in the desert but also to apply the technological principles of run-off irrigation to the whole of the Near Eastern desert.

CONCLUDING STATEMENT

During the last hundred years, American archaeology has provided the scientific community with an awareness of the wide range of human cultural histories in America and in many other parts of the world. It has recovered quantifiable data from which more sophisticated analyses of long-term culture change can be made, not only by archaeologists but by other social scientists as well. It has continually laid a broader base for the comprehensive understanding of the total cultural history of man, including the beginnings of culture, the overall outlines of its development, and the processes that conditioned it.

5
LINGUISTIC ANTHROPOLOGY

Relationships among languages are a major line of evidence of relationships among peoples and cultures. In field work in another culture, command of a community's language is indispensable to recording and understanding its ways of life. Differences in content and the use of language may indicate differences in thought and behavior; sameness may indicate something of a common human nature. The ways linguists analyze the structure of a language may show how to analyze other aspects of culture. For these and other reasons linguistic research is an established branch of anthropology in the United States.

Language, of course, is studied by many disciplines, ranging from the philologist deciphering an ancient text and the critic assessing poetic style to the psychologist measuring word associations or perception of sounds. All such study ultimately contributes to a general field called linguistics; but, as the examples indicate, differences in the material studied, and in the questions asked, have given rise to a number of distinct traditions. Linguistics proper commonly describes languages, classifies them, and explains their differences and similarities. Linguistic research in anthropology shares these concerns, but is shaped by the circumstances in which anthropologists work, the problems on which they focus, and the need for each part of anthropology to relate to the others. And whereas linguists may be able to limit their concern to features of language studied for their own sake, anthropologists must inevitably address themselves to the use and meaning of linguistic phenomena in the lives of those among whom they are found. The functions of speaking are of as much concern as the structures of language. In general, then, linguistic anthropology is the study of speech and language within the context of anthropology.

The contributions and needs of linguistic anthropology can be considered in terms of two major areas: linguistic change and history, and linguistics in the study of contemporary societies and cultures.

LINGUISTIC CHANGE AND HISTORY

The student of prehistory wishes to trace the movements and contact of peoples and the development and diffusion of features of culture; in general, to discover the unrecorded history of mankind and whatever regularities may underlie it. Linguistic research is essential to these goals. The existence of a relationship between two languages may pose an otherwise unsuspected historical problem: it is first of all on linguistic grounds, for example, that we know that the original home of the Navaho of New Mexico and Arizona must be sought in the far northwest of Canada and Alaska. Classification of languages may clarify an historical process: linguistic grounds make it clear that the expansion of Bantu speakers over southern Africa must be recent. Often it is possible to infer something of the detailed cultural history of peoples: the English word for "wine" can be shown to have been borrowed from Latin before the Anglo-Saxons invaded the British Isles, and thus to imply their knowledge of wine somewhere in continental Europe at that early date. From a comparative analysis of Sanskrit, Greek, Latin, and other languages, it is possible to reconstruct the earlier existence of a patrilineal, pastoral people who worshipped a sky-god.

The great triumph of linguistic science in the nineteenth century was to demonstrate that the languages of the Irish, English, Greeks, Russians, Romans, and most other peoples of Europe, together with those of the Persians and the ancient conquerors of India, have a common origin as members of what we now call the Indo-European language family. Work on Indo-European languages has developed the first secure methods for showing languages to be related through common descent, for detecting words borrowed into one language from another, and for reconstructing features of the language and culture of an earlier time.

Linguists working in the context of anthropology have tested the methods developed with Indo-European languages and have shown them to be general in application. They have created the comparative study of language families such as Algonquian (Delaware, Menominee, Blackfoot, Cheyenne, and others), Athapaskan (Navaho, Apache, Hupa, and others), Siouan (Omaha, Crow, Dakota, and others), and others, alongside comparative Indo-European. There are, however, important qualifications. Indo-European is not typical of the cases confronting anthropologists. For most of the Indo-European languages there are detailed grammars and dictionaries; moreover, the investigator usually speaks at least one of the languages and has studied several of them in school. Earlier stages of some of the languages are attested by documents. And in any case the common origin of the languages lies not much more than 6,000 years in the past.

In contrast, anthropologists do not usually have prior knowledge of the languages whose prehistory is of concern to them and must rely on recorded data that are often quite incomplete—sometimes consisting only of a word list. Earlier stages are usually not attested by documents and the relationships of interest often go back much farther than 6,000 years (the origin of American Indians in Asia, for example, is a matter of at least 12,000 years). On both counts, then —limited description and greater erosion of time—the anthropologist must often work with bodies of data far less substantial than those familiar to the student of Indo-European.

Two responses are made. The first is intensive descriptive work, to provide grammars and dictionaries that can support penetration of the remote past. Such work reflects a permanent crisis of linguistic anthropology: to rescue knowledge of languages about to disappear, the one task that later generations of scientists cannot perform for themselves. A description salvaged today makes possible a variety of scientific studies for many generations to come. And often such work is sought out by descendants of those who spoke the languages; for many people anthropology becomes a custodian of their heritage from the past.

The second response is experimentation and innovation in methodology. Mathematical and statistical analyses are used to prove historical relationship among languages, and to estimate the degree of age of such relationship. A small sector of vocabulary ("basic vocabulary") has been defined, characterized as that portion of vocabulary whose meanings are found in all or nearly all languages (e.g., common body parts, natural phenomena such as sun, rock, water, wood, first and second person singular pronouns), which persist over time, and which is impervious to replacement by borrowing from other languages. Its properties are being explored, including its tendency to show a constant rate of change. Computer processing of the large bodies of data involved in far-flung relationships is being developed and a beginning has been made on experimental study of what one can hope to establish of the history of languages recorded only in modern times. The power of different kinds and amounts of evidence can be investigated by comparing what could be established about the history of languages like English and French if one knew only their present form, with what in fact we know about them through long documentation and from other related languages. Work has also begun on formalization of the inference of the original homeland of a group of languages from their present locations and on formalization of the procedures by which one infers the meanings in the parent language of each of a set of semantically related words, given their present meanings. In sum, the foundations of linguistic prehistory are being made an object of basic research.

These newer methods contribute to a grasp of the relationships of languages over larger stretches of space and time, to a systematic theory of the nature of such relationships, and to the methods of their study. There is even the hope of demonstrating the common origin of most or all of the languages of mankind. Traditional methods of work remain indispensable. In demonstrating what features of a language have been borrowed, in discriminating their relative age, in delineating the interrelationships of a group of dialects or languages, in reconstructing features of an earlier stage of a language or an earlier stage common to a group of languages, there are many particular assessments and inferences as to detail. Moreover, the more recent the period with which one is concerned, the richer the material with which one has to work; the interconnections between linguistic prehistory and the rest of history, while potentially more precise, are also more intricate. This kind of work requires a close control of data that only years of experience with a group of languages and cultures can produce—an expertise in Algonquian or Polynesian, say, comparable to that of a specialist in Germanic. The same is true if hypotheses as to the nature of linguistic change, both as something dependent on general characteristics of the human mind and as something interdependent with cultural change, are to be tested.

It is in these respects—laying a descriptive foundation, exploring more remote relationships, conducting research into methodological foundations, providing expert competence for exotic language groups (for prehistoric and for other research)—that the anthropological tradition makes its contribution.

The historical findings of linguistics are depended on by scientists in other fields. A new classification of the languages of Africa, for example, has had a major impact on the general conception of the relations among African cultures. Other consequences of the same importance may be expected as greater scope and precision are reached in study of the languages of the Americas, the Pacific, and Asia (and Africa as well). Whether the Malayo-Polynesians spread through the Pacific from New Guinea or from the mainland of Asia, whether the Melanesians represent the conquering of once independent Negro groups by Malayo-Polynesians, whether some American Indians came to or from Pacific islands—these are kinds of questions to which linguistic findings are crucial.

Such findings affect the very organization of knowledge about the peoples and cultures of the world. The fit between linguistic and other boundaries, of the linguistic and other relationships among peoples, is not perfect; indeed, interesting problems (to be noted later) arise from that fact. To a great extent, however, classification and study of the relationships among peoples has required and continues to require classification and study of relationships among languages as well—a fact reflected in frequent reference to the "ethnolinguistic" groups of an area (such as Southeast Asia). The specialist in an area must know its linguistic relationships. These relationships are important as well to the scientist who wishes to test hypotheses as to causal relationships (between, say, an economic practice and a form of social relationship). He may need a sample of cases that have developed independently, and linguistic relationships are a factor in choosing the sample.

It should be made clear that the study of linguistics and the study of other forms of cultural change are interdependent. Although linguistics has been discussed here in terms of what it offers other fields, the relationships are in fact reciprocal. Many linguistic problems require extralinguistic knowledge. One must take archaeology, ethnology, and social history into account, as to location and movement of peoples, kinds of contact among them, probable kinds of meanings and changes of meaning in given cultures, and so forth. One needs to know, for example, the provenience and composition over time of the populations among whom the several Caribbean Creoles developed; whether or not a group in Polynesia could have been in communication with a group in Mexico before Columbus; whether the social conditions for pidginization of language might have been present in India after the Aryan conquest; whether among Pacific Coast Indians a word for "dog" could also have meant generically "meat," or "toward the house" also "toward the water."

More generally, linguistic change is part of the process of social and cultural change. It has been said that the goal of anthropology is to explain the similarities and differences among mankind. There are four broad explanations for the features and structures present in a language (apart from those inherent in the nature of mankind and language): retention, diffusion, drift, and adaptation. English is what it is partly because of what it retains from an ancestral stage that we call proto-Germanic (beyond that, proto-Indo-European); because of the influence of other languages, especially French; and because of trends internal to its structures. English resembles or differs from other languages (and survives to be studied) also because of the use that has been made of it: it has been the language of the English, in England, and subsequently, of Canadians, Americans, Australians, and others in certain other parts of the world; it has been, successively, the language of a Germanic "tribe," a feudal kingdom, a national state, and an empire and network of trade; it has become a language of world literature, philosophy, and science, and has had its resources developed for these various purposes. Swahili is what it is because of its Bantu origin, the influence of other languages, especially Arabic, and its own internal developments, but also because it is a lingua franca, and second language, for members of particular societies in a particular part of the world.

Many facts about retention, diffusion, and drift can be established with linguistic data alone. But to explain their causes or to understand the development of a language as a whole, especially through adaptation, requires the broader scope of anthropology and the other social sciences.

This point has special importance in the modern world. Throughout much of human history a major force for linguistic change has been the separation and movement of peoples—the dispersal of the original Indo-Europeans, the peopling of the New World. This kind of change—diversification (and the retracing of its path)—first dominated scientific thought. Knowledge about this kind of change and methods for analyzing it are most highly developed. Today and in the future the major forces for linguistic change will have to do with the mingling of peoples and the reintegration of diverse languages, their mutual adaptation, within cities, nations, regions, and indeed the world. The linguistic acculturation of American Indian tribes; the emergence of pidgin and creole languages in Africa, the Caribbean, and the Pacific; the decline of local dialects in Europe; the development of new languages of education, government, and national identity in Africa and Asia; and the changing patterns and valuations of pronunciation in American communities are all a part of the emergence of a world industrial society. The social motivation for such change is clear, but knowledge and methods for studying it and for explaining convergence and adaptation are not well developed. To fill that gap poses one of the great challenges to linguistic research. The anthropologist has a special opportunity to contribute by combining linguistics with social analysis. Just that combination is needed to help answer many questions, both practical and theoretical. The practical relevance to language policy in developing nations and to education is especially clear. The most general theoretical goal is to explain the nature of the interdependence of linguistic and social change. In the study of remote change, the results of both linguistics and social analysis can be brought into relation and the methods of their study compared, but only in the study of recent and current change is it possible to study the process itself. Only there can one directly examine both language and culture, and develop an integrated method for their study. Here, then, is a major area of study in which theoretical and practical needs coincide.

Most study of linguistic change in anthropology has been within the context of prehistory, but the study of linguistic change as an aspect of modern history is beginning to emerge. Both kinds of study require an integration of linguistic and other social science training and research that is rare today in the United States, since it cuts across conventional boundaries and specializations. Special programs will be needed to develop an adequate cadre of specialists.

LINGUISTICS IN SOCIAL-CULTURAL ANTHROPOLOGY

Linguistics is part of the study of contemporary societies and cultures (ethnography) as a practical tool, as a source of methodological insight, and as a form of inquiry in its own right.

Fieldwork Skills

Practical use of a language may be needed for survival; certainly it is necessary for adequate work. One's command of the local language determines the extent to which one can interview persons privately, catch insights from overheard remarks, and participate in revealing conversations. Reliance on interpreters or translators limits the information that can be obtained in a natural way, and knowledge of the local language still is needed as a control. The language can often not be studied in advance, at least not the local dialect, and since continued study will be needed in the field in any case, linguistic training is essential. It prepares the field worker to notice, record, and analyze features of pronunciation, grammar, and meaning—for practical mastery and as part of his data.

The minimal level of skill required of an ethnographer consists of transcription, translation, and the analysis that goes into the making of a lexical and grammatical file. This level of analysis is itself a valuable source of knowledge. Some ethnographers have the training to provide full-scale descriptions (grammar, texts, and dictionary). In any case, a minimal level of skill is necessary to the essential task of obtaining and analyzing native terminology and to discuss whatever aspect of culture is under study. Such verbal data reflects a partial analysis of the aspect of culture by the people themselves, and a partial condensation of its meaning; both are indispensable to questioning in depth.

Some ethnographic research is in itself linguistic research. This may be the case at any time when verbal data pose problems of analysis that go beyond the grammar and lexicon at hand. It is especially the case when speech and meaning are central to the work. Something must thus be said about linguistic methodology, since so much ethnographic research depends on it and, at the same time, extends and corrects it.

Methodological Insight

Linguistic methodology makes important contributions to anthropology beyond the ordinary study of language. First, language is a specially advantageous area in which to study the nature of culture as a whole. Second, the methods of linguistics have suggested ways to analyze other cultural phenomena. Especially since World War II, the success of linguistics in discovering structural regularities and in providing formal (explicit, precise) accounts of them has inspired emulation. There have been attempts to transfer a linguistic model literally to other phenomena, and attempts simply to analyze other phenomena on the same methodological principles as linguistics. The one approach looks for structures resembling structures already known from language; the other seeks the structures (of whatever appearance) that the basic principles justify. Efforts of the first sort have proven abortive, while those of the second have had a continuing influence.

The major influences, briefly put, have been the principles of *contrast* and of *rule-governed creativity* (or adaptation). The first points to the discovery of structural elements and patterns, the second to the discovery of the relations of observed elements and patterns to implicit ones.

The principle of *structural contrast* has emerged in the study of speech sounds, the sector of language on which modern linguistics first focused. It was soon realized that speech sounds have a place in

a covert mental pattern, or model, and that their effective status depends, not merely on their physical properties, but also on whether
or not substitution of one for another in a given context does or
does not make an utterance a different sentence (or no sentence at
all) in the language in question. Thus, raising the back of the tongue
from its position between *b* and *t* in *boot* to that in *boat* can change
one sentence to another in English, as in "I gave her the ——."
Prolonging the vowel of *boot* does not change the sentence (so far
as what can be called the "referential" meaning of the sentence is
concerned). In many of the world's languages (e.g., Siuslaw, formerly
spoken on the Oregon coast) the opposite is true; prolongation of *oo*
could make a different sentence, change of height between *oo* and *oa*
could not.

It is in terms of this principle of contrast—discovering which features are part of the system and make a difference to speakers of a
language—that the regularities in languages can first be found and
the behavior of speakers of a language predicted. One can, for example, anticipate how words from a language of a different system of
contrasts will be heard, and, if borrowed, pronounced. English *boat*
becomes *puut* ("poot") in Siuslaw (which also does not contrast *b*
to *p*).

The second principle, that of *rule-governed creativity* (or generative relations), is needed to deal with the relations into which con-
trastively relevant units enter. Units can be classified into sets according to the positions in which they occur; and the arrangement or
order of these sets relative to one another can be described. For a
time many linguists studied the relations among units primarily in
terms of such observable patterns. More recently the severe limitations of such purely "distributional" analysis has become clear. Such
analysis treats as like sentences that are different, and treats separately sentences that belong together. "The shooting of the blacks
was terrible" shows a single set of words in a single order, but representing two sentences. The blacks may be on either end of the gun;
that is, there are two different relationships of the noun "blacks" to
the gerund "shooting" (object in the one case, subject in the other).
Conversely, "Zellig refused the honor," "The honor was refused by
Zellig," and "Did Zellig refuse the honor?" are three distinct types of
overt sentence (active, passive, and interrogative); yet, if given one

of them, a competent speaker of English can easily supply the others. A common relationship runs through all three.

Facts such as these show that occurring sentences are the manifestation, sometimes convergent and sometimes divergent, of a rich covert system of relationships and meanings. The full structure and interpretation of a sentence depends on its participation in this implicit system. For most linguists today the central problem is how best to account for the complex relations of occurring sentences to the underlying system (deep structure).

The principle of contrast can be said to focus on discovering which elements are relevant and valid, the principle of generative relationships on which uses of elements are relevant and valid. For the linguist, the central question is to discover and explain what is grammatical and ungrammatical. For the ethnographer, there is the larger question of what is appropriate and inappropriate, including sometimes the use of a particular language or any language at all. Both share a concern to deal with kinds of knowledge that users of a language have and their ability to use that knowledge in creative, adaptive ways.

ETHNOGRAPHIC SEMANTICS

The principles just discussed have been extended to the analysis of cultural patterns, particularly of kinship systems, mythology (where important new discoveries have been made), ceremonial behavior, material culture, terminology for aspects of the natural environment, and some aspects of interpersonal communication. Names vary: in kinship the approach is often called "componential analysis"; in mythology, "structural analysis"; with regard to interpersonal communication, "ethnography of speaking," or sociolinguistics. If considered as aspects of ethnographic semantics, all can be said to be concerned to discover and explain the kinds of knowledge that members of a culture have by determining how that knowledge is linguistically classified, stored, retrieved, and used. Not all knowledge is classified in this way, but large and crucial portions are, making ethnographic semantics fundamental to many other kinds of inquiry and to many kinds of practical work, such as attempts to introduce new knowledge and procedures to a culture.

The initial task is always the structural one—determining the implicit question (or frame of reference) to which an utterance or other action is one of a set of alternative answers, to discover the membership of the set, and to discover the dimensions (or features) that define the alternatives. It is extremely important not to impose an incorrect question, set, or dimension. There are many universal aspects of semantic structure, but in any given case one must be prepared to be surprised. Color is often assumed to be a universal category for words, but among the Hanunoo of the Philippines words we translate into English as color terms belong to a set that answers a more general question about visual appearance. One major underlying dimension is colorimetric; the other has to do with "wetness" and "dryness" (reflecting a concern with succulence, ripeness, freshness, dryness, etc. in a pervasively botanical world). Thus universality is to be found in elementary dimensions and features; relativity of different cultural experiences and adaptations enters into the particular features and combinations of features chosen for expression. Hanunoo has color as a semantic dimension, but not as a set of words.

Many difficulties of translation are of just this sort. A word in one language may have no equivalent, as a word, in another; but if analyzed as a set of semantic features, the word may be perfectly clear. In the Sedang language of Vietnam there is a set of particles that students find almost impossible to grasp as words until analysis shows them to be members of a set organized in part in terms of the contrast between affirmation—negation, on the one hand, and past —nonpast time on the other. The underlying dimensions are intelligible and universal, but uniting them into single words is distinctively Sedang and at first opaque.

Meaning is usually analyzed in terms of "reference," what is talked about, but it obviously depends also on "expression," how something is said. Those features not used to distinguish reference can be used to convey attitude, identity, or other social meanings. In English, changing the vowel of *boat* to that of *boot* changes the topic; prolonging the vowel of *boat* changes the way something is said about the topic (as in "She gave me the boat," "She gave me the boot,"

"She gave me the *boat*, not *boot*, silly"). Conversely, in a language in which change of length changes the reference of a word, it is change in the quality of the vowel (such as from *oo* to *oa* in Siuslaw) that can express emphasis. The particular expressive meaning depends on the relation between the stylistic feature and the reference, as in the effect of the soft sounds in Tennyson's "The murmuring of innumerable bees in immemorial elms." The slight change of the fourth word to "enumerable" spoils the music and hence the picture.

These two functions, the "referential" and the "expressive," exist in tight interdependence at all levels of language and in all modes of communication. The expressive component of meaning has been less well explored, methods for recording and analyzing it less well established. However, to explain the meaning of verbal messages and the role of languages in the lives of those who use them requires grasping the interplay between language and that part of a message our ordinary orthography does not allow us to write down—the part comprised of use of voice, gesture, eye, and body. The practical utility of this kind of cross-cultural knowledge is apparent.

Some intensive work has been done, and special names created for it—paralinguistics (analyses of the nonlinguistic features of voice), kinesics (concerned with gesture and body motion), and proxemics (the study of handling spatial relationships). There are only a handful of trained workers, however, and research has been done largely in the United States. For any substantial advance the number of researchers must be multiplied and the small cadre of qualified persons brought together to train them for the extensive ethnography that is needed.

Most work in expressive communication has been directed toward identifying relevant units. The principle of contrast often discovers here not discrete units, as in ordinary language structure, but polarities, scales, and continua (e.g., in intonations). How to identify the social meaning of expressive features and how to integrate them with the rest of communication is hardly known. Generative relations to an underlying structure must exist. Different modalities may express the same underlying message (either a "yes" or a nod to signify assent); and the same overt sequence may have different underlying meaning, depending on the relationship among modalities (e.g., "Just what I wanted" said with vocal surprise, or sarcasm, or with different accompanying gestures). One of the main challenges in efforts to analyze language as part of social life is the development of explicit models of these relations.

Two other spheres in which contrast and generative relations are essential are discourse and acts of speech. *Discourse* may represent here the more formalized genres—myth, folktale, proverb, sermon, and the like, as well as the informal discourse of conversation. Linguistic analysis has always been necessary to the study of discourse. There is now great interest in discovering structural units and sequences of a linguistic sort and generative rules that derive different versions of a myth or different styles from one underlying structure. Such work extends linguistics "horizontally," as it were, going beyond the sentence to the text. Study of *speech acts* is a "vertical" extension. The same interrogative sentence may be either a request or an instruction (e.g., "Isn't it ten o'clock?" either to an adult or to a child who should be in bed). Different sentence forms may be functionally equivalent—"Isn't it ten o'clock?" and "Time to go to bed" as alternative instructions. Such facts imply a level of structure deeper than the sentence. The nature of this level of speech act (requests, commands, instructions, admonitions, greetings, and so forth), and its interdependence with sentence forms are only beginning to be explored.

Discourse and speech acts are ideal topics of linguistic ethnography, for they require knowledge of both linguistics and culture. With both topics the major concern now is to ground analysis adequately in social context. Students of genres such as myth are turning from analysis of texts in and of themselves to analysis of texts as shaped in the interaction between speaker and audience. The status of a sentence form as a speech act obviously depends on social relationship and setting. To address someone by a title and last name may be ingratiating, courteous, or insulting, depending on the relations normally obtaining between the parties. ("Professor Jones," for example, as said by someone who need not, should or should not, e.g. his wife, use the form in question.) Exploration of these relationships tightens the interdependence of linguistics and enthnography in three ways. First, the areas of common data and method are extended. With forms of address, for example, one may analyze the meaning of the forms and the character of the relationships and settings in terms of the same dimensions and formal schema—features of social distance, formality vs. informality, relative status and authority. Second, the required ethnographic analysis serves as a corrective and support for purely linguistic analysis. When linguistic analysis is based on the judgments of acceptability made by speakers, difficulty and confusion can be escaped only if the judgments are controlled for situational context and social background. Third, it becomes apparent that there is a broad new area of phenomena that must be explored in common. The interdependence of linguistic and social factors within the speech event leads to a recognition of speaking as a structured activity.

Linguists have usually extracted from speech just those regularities specific to grammar. Ethnographers have usually abstracted just that information revealing of broad patterns of social structure and cultural values. Each has left explicit analysis of speaking to the other. The proprieties of who can say what to whom, when and where, in what way, with what means, to what purpose; the meaning of choice of one or another way of speaking; the place of language relative to other modes of communication; how a child acquires knowledge and competence with regard to all these things—these matters have only been touched upon, never focused upon and deeply explored. It is in this area, the ethnography of speaking or sociolinguistics, that work must be done if the foundations for an understanding of the place of language in human life are ever to be adequately laid.

The practical implications are great for understanding other societies and for understanding problems in our own urban centers and schools. On the one hand, it is the difference between knowing a language and knowing how to use it. A child acquires both kinds of knowledge together. He acquires not only grammar, but also attitudes towards the use of language; he acquires the meanings, not only of words, but also of acts of speech. Much misunderstanding abroad and in our own society stems from ignorance of this fact. Teachers, for example, may not know that styles of speaking that are normal for them are interpreted as hostile and threatening by Indian children. Children from minority groups may be judged taciturn and relatively nonverbal when only certain situations, those of interaction with superiors, are observed. It may not be noticed that outside those situations the children are as verbal as any others, and even, as in the case of many black children, usually sensitive to art and skill in speech. Again, it may be wondered why poor black children, seeing as much television as middle-class white children, and hearing white teachers all day, continue to speak differently. One finding that is already clear is that it is not quantity of exposure, but identification with others, that is decisive in linguistic change. Often enough the black children can, if they wish to, adopt the desired standard style in play. Superficial features of pronunciation and grammar are often taken as evidence of intellectual ability or lack of ability. Attention is often concentrated negatively on such points and the effect is to discourage, rather than encourage, the use of the desired form of speech.

One needs to know what the alternative ways of speaking in a community are and the use and meaning of each. On that basis one can judge what problems will arise from introducing or using a different way of speaking. The description of ways of speaking, however, cuts across the usual work of linguists and ethnographers. In short, efforts to devise policies for cities and schools, like efforts to devise language policies in multilingual nations or to conduct valid cross-cultural research despite language differences, are attempting to apply a basic science that has only begun to be built.

6
PHYSICAL ANTHROPOLOGY

Physical anthropologists are particularly interested in the biological aspects of anthropological problems. Their long-term evolutionary problems are concerned with such subjects as the separation of man and ape, origin of bipedal locomotion, and the relation of tools to biological change. In the solution of this kind of problem the anthropologist seeks the active assistance of the geologist, paleontologist, and the student of evolution. The short-term problems are those which attempt to interpret the biological variations among contemporary peoples. It is here that the major effort of physical anthropology has been, and continues to be, made. Traditionally, variation was studied in anatomical terms (skeletal form, hair, color, and so forth) and particularly by measurement. Recently there has been emphasis on features of known genetic origin (blood groups and hemoglobin variants, for example). Biometry has been greatly strengthened by the advent of computers. Here the physical anthropologist turns to medical science and to the statistician. The importance of the long-term evolutionary problems is primarily philosophical; they help to give an understanding of man's place in nature and of the process of evolution. The short-term studies have the same objective, plus many practical applications, as in the study of schoolchildren's growth for use in the sizing of uniforms and other equipment.

In the following pages the emphasis will be on recent developments, particularly those which affect planning for adequate manpower and more effective teaching and research.

MAN'S PLACE IN NATURE

Recent discoveries support the point of view stated many years ago that the chimpanzee and gorilla are man's closest living relatives. The study of chromosomes, DNA, or albumin leads to the same conclusion, and there is high hope that biochemical studies now in progress will not only prove the relationship, but also provide methods of estimating when the human lineage separated from that of contemporary apes. Present estimates of how long the human lineage has been separate vary from five to thirty million years! Direct evidence about the length of the separation and about the structure of our ancestors must come from the fossil record, and numerous discoveries are being made at the present time, especially through the efforts of L. S. B. Leakey and E. L. Simons. Unfortunately, the remains discovered thus far are so fragmentary that competent specialists disagree on their interpretation.

The nature of the differences between man and the nonhuman primates is being revealed by field studies. George B. Schaller (1963) observed gorillas for nearly a year, and Jane van Lawick-Goodall (1967) has followed the life of chimpanzees in Tanzania for over seven years. These studies reveal our nearest animal relatives as intensely social and very different from the savage creatures pictured by the travelers of the nineteenth century. In many phases of its behavior (use of objects, throwing stones, some hunting, for example) the chimpanzee appears to be the most human of the contemporary primates. The field studies give essential information on group size and organization, mother-infant relationships, peer groups, play and exploration, dominance and group protection; these topics are also being investigated in laboratories under controlled conditions. The systematic combination of field observations under natural conditions and imaginative experiment is beginning to afford a new kind of understanding into primate nature and the evolution of man.

In summary, our understanding of man's place in nature is being

enriched by field studies of the behavior of the contemporary primates, the discovery of new fossils, and by a wide range of experiments
and laboratory techniques.

MAN-APES AND MAN'S EARLIEST ANCESTORS

Whatever our precise relationship with the apes (*Pon-
gidae*) may be, by about four million years ago our ancestors were
bipedal, tool-using creatures with brains no larger than those of the
contemporary apes. When the first of these small-brained men was
described by Raymond Dart, most scientists thought that the form
was an ape because of the small size of the brain. It took many
finds before scientists realized that the large brain of man (genus
Homo) was an end product of human evolution that appeared long
after bipedalism, small teeth, tool-making, hunting, and many other
human attributes.

Man-Apes: The Genus Australopithecus

Documentation of this very early stage of human evolution is due primarily to discoveries by Raymond Dart, L. S. B.
Leakey, John Robinson, and the late Robert Broom. Of the many
fossils found in Africa, the teeth and skull are usually well preserved, but the remainder of the skeleton is represented only by
fragmentary remains. Thus technical controversy continues on how
many different kinds of man-apes existed and which one may have
been the ancestor of later forms of man. Many fossils, beginning
with those discovered by Robert Broom in 1936, have been assigned
to the genus *Australopithecus*, which was originally defined by Raymond Dart in 1925. Later fossil finds (contemporary with *Australopithecus*) have sometimes been assigned other names, but the
debates over these relationships need not concern us here. The implications for human evolution are clear, regardless of the controversial
details.

One persistent problem in the study of evolution is determining the
age of fossils. The cave deposits of South Africa, where most of the
man-ape fossils have been found, are particularly difficult to date.

Fortunately, in East Africa man-ape fossils are found in strata of volcanic origin which can be dated by radiometric methods like potassium-argon determinations. This method shows that the man-apes were fully evolved by about four million years ago and persisted until approximately six or seven hundred thousand years ago. These data strongly suggest that our ancestors were small-brained, tool-using bipeds for several millions of years before the appearance of the genus *Homo*.

Homo Erectus

Java has yielded the earliest remains of men of our genus. Teuku Jacob is now continuing the explorations started by Eugene Du Bois in the 1880s and by G. H. R. von Koenigswald in the 1930s. We now have fragments of seven Java men, and new excavations should soon increase the number. The most complete series of *Homo erectus*—Peking man—was lost during World War II. This stage of human evolution is represented by fossils from Africa[1] and Europe as well as from the Far East, by countless stone tools, and by the bones of the animals killed by our ancestors. At least some of them used fire and their brains were twice the size of those of the man-apes. During the period from 600,000 to 50,000 years ago there seems to have been very little evolution in the locomotor skeleton, but the brain increased in size by something on the order of 40 per cent.

Unfortunately, with very rare exceptions, the only tools preserved from this immense interval of time are made of stone. Most of the tools actually used were probably of wood, and archaeologists find it exceedingly difficult to determine how the stones were used. No doubt there was substantial biological and cultural evolution during these hundreds of thousands of years. Newer methods of dating and analysis will yield the answers to many of the questions.

Homo Sapiens

By 50,000 years ago the populations of ancient men had evolved into forms very similar to those alive today. The fossil men

[1] During much of the last million years approximately half of the world suitable for human occupation was in Africa.

of Europe and comparable races in other parts of the Old World had large ridges of bone on their brows and some few other features that differentiate them from ourselves, but the differences, at least to the extent that they show in the skeleton, are minor. Later populations show characters intermediate between the ancient men and anatomically modern man. By 35,000 b.c., all fossils are indistinguishable from the bones of contemporary people. Anthropologists differ widely on the nature of events during the transitional period. Some stress geographic separation and believe in a relatively independent parallel evolution from ancient men into modern races. Others argue persuasively that there was a much greater gene flow among the populations of the genus *Homo*. The differences are due in part to theoretical considerations, but more importantly to insufficient data. For example, until recently there were no early skeletons from India. Obviously, the degree of separation between East and West cannot be determined without knowledge of the intermediate populations.

CULTURE AS A FACTOR
IN HUMAN EVOLUTION

The direction of evolution is determined by successful adaptation; in the case of man, tools and the diverse ways of life they make possible have dominated evolution for about four million years. Human evolution has been a feedback relationship leading to increasingly complex and diversified ways of life. In contrast to the way of life of monkeys and apes, the human way depends on skill, cooperation, division of labor, political organization, family, religion, and the arts. The earliest fundamental contrast between ape and human adaptation is the importance of tools in human adaptation. Another important distinction lies in the fact that all phases of human adaptation now depend on language. Without language no complex social life would be possible. Apes cannot be taught to talk, but men learn language, any language, so easily that the acquisition of language is inevitable under normal circumstances. This ability depends on large areas of the brain. Unfortunately for the student of evolution, the brain leaves no clear mark on the skull that might signify the presence of linguistic ability. However, starting from linguistic data, Eric H. Lenneberg estimates that contemporary languages date back 30,000 to 50,000 years, to the time when populations of ancient men were evolving into populations of modern men. This period seems to have been one in which the slow change of the ancient world accelerated into what we now regard as normal, and language may have been a major factor in this transformation. In the period between 30,000 and 10,000 years ago (only 20,000 years of the 600,000 years that the genus *Homo* has existed!), man invented boats, occupied Australia, the Arctic, and the New World (doubling the area for human occupation), invented the bow and many new tools, and domesticated the dog and finally plants and other animals. This revolution in the way of life first permitted the human occupation of the whole world (except the polar regions) and the differentiation of the Australian aborigines, the American Indians, and, much later, the people of Oceania. New ways of life—especially for food production—led to great increases in population and to movements of populations and changed the history of disease. For more than 99 per cent of the duration of the genus *Homo* our ancestors were gatherers and hunters; the entire species probably numbered no more than five to ten million people. The recent success of our species depends on technical discoveries, not on biological evolution—although evolution has continued, as will be indicated in the next section.

In summary, the further back in time we go, the more our evolution can be treated as a biological problem similar to that of any other mammal; but the closer we come to the present, the more evolution is dominated by culture, by customs which are learned.

MICROEVOLUTION

The study of human races has always been the predominant activity of physical anthropologists, but emphasis has shifted from classification and the reconstruction of history to the attempt to understand process.

The traditional studies only considered phenotypical characters of unknown genetic background (stature, cephalic index, hair form, and so forth). While these interests have continued, recent investigations are primarily concerned with interpreting the distribution of traits of known genetic origin (such as blood groups and biochemical variations). Emphasis on genetics gives a clarification and extension to evolutionary thinking. The clarification comes from the removal of methods and theories that are incompatible with genetics (like orthogenesis, vitalism, and particularly in anthropology, extreme typological thinking). The extension comes from an interest in many new traits and the possibility of using mathematical models when the genetic basis for the traits is known.

The change from the traditional mode of thinking is perhaps best shown by the analysis of mixtures between human populations. Traditionally, the characteristics of many human populations (Bushmen, Australian aborigine, American Indian, to name only a few) were attributed to mixtures. But when the blood groups and other traits of known genetic background were studied, the characteristics of not a single population could be accounted for by the postulated mixtures. The gene frequencies not only showed that the postulated mixtures did not account for the observed situations, but also that other factors in addition to mixture must have been operating.

Genetics has clarified both theory and method in the study of the microevolution of man. A well-understood case is one in which a disease—malaria—has affected gene frequencies. Three red blood cell polymorphisms (sickling trait, thalassemia, and glucose-6-phosphate dehydrogenase deficiency) give some measure of protection against malaria; their distributions are determined in part by the survival of those resistant to the disease. Human agricultural customs increased the incidence of mosquitoes and the malaria they carried, and set the genetic evolution into motion; now mosquito control is reducing the incidence of malaria and hence changing the adaptive value of the protective genes. It is the hope of many scientists that the meaning of many other gene frequencies will be understood in comparable ways. The interrelations of biology, customs, and disease offer fascinating and practical areas for future research.

CLIMATIC ADAPTATION

Anthropologists and many other scientists have long been interested in the relation of climate to the structure of the body. The early crude correlations, often coupled with notions of the inheritance of acquired characters, have been replaced by careful statistical and experimental investigations. While there is no doubt that most of man's adaptation is by his culture, there remains a question as to what extent some of his biology may be an adaptation to climatic conditions. It should be remembered that many of the differences between contemporary populations have a substantial antiquity and that direct biological adaptation to climatic differences may have been much more important during the preagricultural existence of our genus. Evidence of adaptation to heat, to cold, to altitude, and to ultraviolet light includes the temperature of men working nude (differing from one group to another), circulation to fingers, body build and possible face form, number of red cells and quantity of blood, size of chest, skin pigment, and thickness of the epidermis. The problem in interpreting the data comes from the fact that man is highly adaptable biologically and much climatic adaptation may thus be made during the lifetime of an individual, frequently in a relatively short period of time. Further research is needed to determine which differences in the adult phenotypes are due to adaptation during the lifetime of an individual and which to underlying genetic differences between populations.

PRACTICAL APPLICATIONS
OF PHYSICAL ANTHROPOLOGY

The most continued application of anthropological techniques has been in the study of human growth. Methods of description, analysis, and interpretation of norms have improved steadily over the years. In World War I measurements were used to help in the production of military uniforms. Unfortunately this effort was not continued between the wars and it was not until World War II that the army anthropometric survey was reestablished.

Since then anthropometry has been used continuously in the armed forces to establish norms for sizes of many items of equipment—uniforms, gloves, shoes, masks, cockpit size, and so forth. The joint efforts of anthropologists and engineers is designed to make the optimum fit between the man and the machine.

The extreme complexity and sophistication of modern equipment and its extraordinary capacities make the dynamic or biomechanical measurements of range, strength, and speed of human movements increasingly important today. Moreover, both static and dynamic measurements must be taken under the conditions to prevail when the equipment is operated: the handle may normally be turned by the gloved hand; the escape hatch may have to accommodate the fully suited pilot wearing his parachute.

Through their studies of modern man and the biological variations among populations, physical anthropologists are uniquely qualified to provide law enforcement agencies with critical descriptive information about human skeletal material discovered under questionable circumstances. Such data as the sex of the deceased and his age at death, certain metrical and morphological characteristics (stature, body build, and even those primary facial features contoured by the underlying bony structure), and racial identity are routinely furnished by anthropologists at the Smithsonian Institution to the Federal Bureau of Identification. During periods of military action, physical anthropological centers undertake the identification of the war dead. In Europe, anthropologists are widely sought by the courts to present evidence on the probable paternity of children or to identify children separated in infancy from their parents during times of social upheaval.

Also of practical importance is the knowledge, accumulating as the result of epidemiological research by physical anthropologists and scientists in related fields, that associates disease incidence and disease immunity with specific populations. The tolerance of some Negroid groups to malaria—the genetic base of which is now understood—has been mentioned. Similarly, the low level of hypertension among the rural Chinese and South African Bantu, as contrasted with Euroamerican groups, is under study by physical and cultural anthropologists; here both biological and cultural factors may play roles. *Kuru,* the progressively debilitating and nearly always fatal muscular disease afflicting certain Eastern Highlands groups in New Guinea, has been intensively studied by physical and cultural anthropologists, jointly with medical researchers; a latent viral infection resulting from cannibalism has been implicated, but aspects of *kuru's* etiology remain mysterious.

Physical anthropologists, after years of close study, have discovered no evidence that racial crossing leads to biological inferiority, as this is usually defined.

Many of these areas of physical anthropological research have as yet been only superficially explored. Nevertheless, it is clear from results obtained so far that exciting discoveries remain to be made in many of these research areas and that many of the findings will possess significant, possibly critically important, practical implications.

7

ANTHROPOLOGY AND
THE PROBLEMS
OF SOCIETY

Anthropology, like other sciences, has a practical as well as a theoretical side. During the past sixty years anthropology has demonstrated its utility in such fields as public health and medicine, agriculture, colonial administration, psychological warfare, education, and community development. Yet in spite of this long and varied experience, the relationships between theoretical and applied anthropology are poorly understood, even within the discipline, and anthropology's full potential in dealing with contemporary society's problems is far from realized. Many anthropologists, for real or imagined ethical reasons, are unwilling to work in programs that are aimed at modifying cultural forms; they still cling to the "thou shalt not tamper" dictum of absolute cultural relativism. Others, for personal reasons of prestige and status, are reluctant to spend time in activities that rate as second class: as in other sciences, contributions to theory outrank contributions to the solutions of social problems. Anthropology's potential as an instrument for enlightened and knowledgeable change is also hampered because the administrators and technical specialists in whose hands the real decision-making power is lodged do not fully comprehend the capacities of social science.

HISTORY

Even among anthropologists, there is still a strong tendency to think of applied anthropology as an exercise in colonial ad-

78

ministration. Few discussions of the subject fail to include an account of the golden stool incident in the Ashanti Wars of the Gold Coast, the most famous and dramatic case in which knowledge of cultural forms and meanings prevented colonial administrators from making a major error in policy. In fact, with very rare exceptions, colonial administration (including the administration of internally marginal peoples such as the United States Indians) *was* the sole focus of applied anthropology, from its inception until the outbreak of World War II. This, of course, has not been true for the past generation. With the end of the colonial system, applied anthropological interest has shifted to the social and cultural problems that accompany technological change and modernization in both industrialized and developing countries. Today most anthropologists who are concerned with the practical aspects of their science deal with the processes of social and cultural change, particularly as they bear upon improving programs in agriculture, health and medical services, educational systems, social welfare, community development, and the like.

The beginning of an applied anthropology depends on the definition of what applied anthropology is. Anthropologists, from the time the discipline emerged as a distinct science, have insisted that it is a "practical" science. Famous anthropologists of the past century, such as E. B. Tylor in Britain and Daniel G. Brinton in the United States, have bequeathed us quotable phrases to prove their point. Yet it is essential to distinguish between such lip service, and the pseudo-scientific anthropology of groups whose members call upon anthropology to "prove" their preconvictions about racial differences, and the systematic use of the scientific method to research social and technical problems and to suggest answers. When anthropologists and anthropologically trained specialists in other fields, including administration, utilize the theoretical concepts, the factual knowledge, and above all, the research methodology of anthropology in programs designed to improve administrative techniques or to ameliorate social, economic, and technological problems, they are engaging in applied anthropology. Defined in this sense, applied anthropology is a product of the present century, about sixty years old. It is perhaps best dated from the 1908 appointment of Northcote W. Thomas as British Government Anthropologist in Nigeria, charged to study the Ibo- and Edo-speaking peoples of that country to facilitate the extension of the then new colonial philosophy of "indirect rule." For the next thirty years almost all applied anthropology dealt with administrative problems and most of it was the product of British anthropologists. Few if any British anthropologists who worked in the Empire in the interwar years failed at one time or another to turn their hand to the problems of colonial administration. Applied anthropology was defined as dealing with native or dependent peoples (such as the American Indians). By this very definition the content of applied anthropology was seen only in terms of understanding the cultures of recipient peoples. The two views reinforced each other, effectively blinding anthropology until a much later date to the importance of understanding in equal degree the social structure, cultural forms, and values of the administrative and innovating organizations.

For want of a colonial empire, few American anthropologists worked in administrative situations, except in Micronesia following World War II, when thirty or more anthropologists researched, and sometimes administered, resettlement and development programs involving the indigenous peoples of these islands. It is true, of course, that Major J. W. Powell, the first chief of the Bureau of American Ethnology (established in 1879), spoke in his first annual report of the importance of his organization's work to the administration of Indian affairs. His comments were perhaps a sop to Congress, which doubtless did not anticipate a purely research-oriented office, for after this early statement, one combs the publications of the bureau in vain for evidence of a practical concern with Indian problems. Some years later the Philippine Ethnological Survey was established (1906–10), apparently modeled after the Bureau of American Ethnology, with the charge of studying the native peoples of America's new colonial outpost. But here again, although by the standards of the times the ethnography was often excellent, the "practical" value appears to have been nil. Real applied anthropological work began in the United States only when the Bureau of Indian Affairs and the Soil Conservation Service joined hands to revitalize the structure and philosophy of the Indian Bureau and to promote conservation measures in the Southwest. Anthropologists who were assigned to the Applied Anthropology Unit worked on such problems as formal leadership and informal government patterns on reservations. They made recommendations on tribal charters and constitutions that were to be introduced. In spite of the high quality of much of their work, anthropologists who participated in these programs feel that they had remarkably little impact on the Indian Bureau and very little effect in improving the situation of the Indian peoples among whom they worked.

During World War II applied anthropology flourished in the United States as anthropologists were drawn into government activities in unprecedented numbers. Many worked in the Community Analysis Section of the War Relocation Authority, which resettled more than 100,000 Japanese from California to camps east of the Sierras. Others worked in the Foreign Morale Division of the Office of War Information, on problems commonly described as "psychological warfare." Still others helped in training officers bound for administrative posts in newly occupied areas, prepared "survival handbooks" telling downed fliers how to live off the land, or helped prepare the "War Background Information" series published by the Smithsonian Institution.

Simultaneously, what may be called "contemporary applied anthropology" was beginning to take shape. This is most clearly seen in the founding of the Society for Applied Anthropology in 1941. From the very first issue of its journal, *Human Organization* (initially *Applied Anthropology*), it is clear that concerned Americans had a very different view of the subject than that which had gone before. The editorial statement of this first issue set the tone (but not the content) that has been followed to the present: the journal was to be "devoted to the solution of practical problems of human relations in the fields of business and political administration, psychiatry, social work and wherever else human relations play a part. It is based upon the premise that a science of human relations can only be developed if theories are tested in practice."

As matters turned out, the surge of developmental efforts in new countries, strongly supported by the American bilateral foreign aid program and the multilateral programs of the United Nations and its specialized agencies, has set the pattern for contemporary applied anthropology. In the postwar years a majority of anthropologists who have devoted time to the practical application of their subject have been concerned with the social aspects of technological change or the human factors in modernization. Anthropologists have been called into developmental programs because they have constructed hypotheses about the integration of society and culture and about the processes of change, and they have developed research methodologies that make it possible for them to provide information about human behavior that is vitally important to the engineer, the planner, and the administrator. Moreover, they share an ethical conviction about intervention in the lives of others and about who plans for whom, which they believe should play a more important role in basic planning than has usually been the case. Some contributions have been simple, as when anthropologists point out to public health officials that latrines with American-style riser seats are unattractive to "squatters" who traditionally go to bushes behind their houses. Others are more complex, as when Mexican anthropologists plan for and supervise the relocation of thousands of Indians whose traditional villages are flooded by new lakes. Some of the reasons that anthropologists' contributions have not been greater are discussed in following sections.

RELATIONSHIPS BETWEEN THEORETICAL AND APPLIED ANTHROPOLOGY

The term "applied anthropology" is an unfortunate misnomer. It suggests that data, theory, and methodology are "applied" in mechanical fashion to contemporary social problems, in much the same way that theoretical knowledge about the properties of gas might be applied to the development of a more efficient refrigerator. "Application" clearly requires a technician or an engineer, but not a top-level scientist. But, as Alvin Gouldner long ago pointed out for the social sciences in general, even in the absence of high-level theory with predictive value about human behavior, we have a healthy applied social science. The reason is clear: in applied social science, including anthropology, our work is described by what Alexander H. Leighton has called a "clinical" rather than an "engineering" model. That is, the applied anthropologist, whose basic training and canons of scientific objectivity are identical to those of his colleagues who work on purely theoretical matters, is in fact in his research usually doing straight, old-fashioned anthropological research. He is not "applying" anything beyond certain basic assumptions about human behavior, a few fundamental concepts like culture, society, status and role, and a research methodology that is flexible and heuristic and that provides him, often, with leads that help him find answers to puzzling questions. In consequence, in most applied work there is as much feedback into the basic corpus of anthropological knowledge as there is from purely theoretical work, just as in medical clinical work there is feedback into the basic corpus of medical knowledge.

The real distinction between theoretical and applied anthropology is not found in anthropology at all, but rather in the bureaucratic structure of research. When an anthropologist selects his own research task, when he is financed by his university or a foundation or government to do what he wants to do, when he has complete control over his research results, and when the principal consumers of his work are his professional colleagues, and perhaps his students, then he is doing "theoretical"—or at least nonpractical—research. But, when the same anthropologist with the same training, the same knowledge, and the same research methodology, works in a program in which the bureaucracy financing the work defines the research topic and has a greater or lesser claim on the anthropologist's research findings, and when these findings are to be used in the solution of "practical" problems, usually of a social-cultural-economic nature, then the anthropologist is doing "applied" work. An important point emerges from this analysis: there really is no such thing as an "applied anthropologist." With exceptions, "applied anthropologist" is a *role* many anthropologists take on from time to time. One is not *either* a research *or* an applied anthropologist; all anthropologists are at least potentially both, and the label that suits each at a particular time is determined by the criteria just mentioned.

ANTHROPOLOGY'S CONTRIBUTIONS TO CONTEMPORARY PROBLEMS

The question is asked: if anthropology does not include theory and data that can be "applied" to practical problems, what, if anything, does it have to offer to the contemporary scene? Most anthropologists feel that their most important contribution to action programs is an unusually broad and flexible field research methodology that is based on a holistic view of society and culture and that uses such general concepts as cultural integration, cultural dynamics, sociocultural systems in contact, and the premises underlying cultural forms as a means to structure research and interpret results. Anthropological research is exploratory and wide-ranging, and in contrast to the more elaborate research methods of other social sciences, it is relatively unstructured. But in directed culture-change programs, where the technical, social, cultural, economic, psychological, and other pertinent factors are almost infinite and usually are not recognized in advance, this exploratory quality is enormously advantageous. It greatly increases the chance that the investigator will discover the critical elements in specific situations, simply because he is trained to search the entire spectrum of the culture he studies.

The concept of "systems" is helpful in understanding the anthropologist's utility to action programs. The anthropologist habitually thinks of data and problems in the context of larger units, which may be social, cultural, or economic, or more likely a combination of these and many more as well. A major part of his task is to define the boundaries of the system that is being affected, so that the outer limits within which data and hypotheses will be considered can be set. In earlier applied anthropological work, these "systems" were tribes or perhaps entire colonies. Today they may be peasant villages, in which health, agricultural, educational, and community-development programs are under way, or—with increasing frequency—minor enclaves in larger societies, such as hospitals, business offices, and bureaucratic administrative organizations.

Whatever the target group, the fundamental point around which anthropological advice is built is that, within any system, when a single trait or element changes, a great many other traits or elements are also bound to change. Or, conversely, in planning change, certain goals cannot be reached except by changing a great many cultural patterns, some of which have no direct connection whatsoever with the narrow—and usually technological—goals of the project. Anthropologists have frequently been helpful in developmental programs because they can point out many of the unforeseen consequences, the secondary and tertiary changes, that will come about inevitably if the primary change is achieved. Often these secondary and tertiary changes have undesirable features that far outweigh the advantages of the primary change, if it can be achieved. Anthropologists, too, by using the same analytical method, can explain why apparently well-designed programs do not produce the desired results.

A new health center is opened in a South American city, modeled on the best United States practice. Attendance is much lower than anticipated. Why? The anthropologist goes from door to door in the area of influence not with a questionnaire, but simply asking if the housewife knows about the center; if she thinks it is useful; if she doesn't take her small children, why not; and a series of similarly general questions. The anthropologist also observes doctors, nurses, and laboratory technicians at work and queries each about his concept of his role. By fitting all the evidence together, a good explanation of underutilization of the center is found, and modifications in procedures significantly increase utilization. Problems include the health center's hours, which are based on the convenience of personnel rather than client; the client's failure to appreciate the Western distinction between curative and preventive medicine; barriers based on class differences between clients and staff; ego-gratification needs of clients and staff; and a host of other items.

THE FOCI OF APPLIED ANTHROPOLOGICAL RESEARCH

In examining the literature of applied anthropology, one is struck by the consistency with which the "problem"—the target of research—is defined as the "native people," the peasant community, the clients of a health center—in a nutshell, the people someone else has decided ought to be better governed, helped, or changed. Whether it is a question of colonial administration or better health practices and services in a low-income American neighborhood, the common assumption is that a professional administrative and technical organization has the knowledge, the wisdom, and the right to make decisions affecting the lives of others—decisions that will result in greater or lesser changes in this way of life—and that it has the mandate and support of the dominant elements in the society that supports the organization to exert every effort to bring about these changes. Whether the goal is improving "indirect rule" or persuading people to brush their teeth morning and evening the underlying structural assumptions are identical.

Given this ethnocentric definition of problem—and anthropologists have shared it—it is not surprising that the anthropologist's role was thought to be learning the social and cultural forms of the "native" peoples or the members of the target group so that programs that "attacked" their problems could be tailored to their cultural forms and phrased in ways consistent with their social structure, all with the goal of more easily "selling" an improved way of life. Underlying this view of applied anthropology is the assumption that in order to achieve success in directed culture-change programs it is essential to know the culture of the group.

In early applied anthropology, especially colonial administration, understanding of the problem did not advance significantly beyond this view. Most of the early applied work in developmental health, agriculture, and education programs also conformed to this model. The model, of course, is not wrong; it is simply deficient. With growing sophistication in identifying directed culture-change problems, we now begin to see that knowledge of the "culture" of the innovating organization, the bureaucratic organization charged with attaining specific goals, is just as important as knowledge of a peasant village. It is perhaps even more important, because it is here that we finally reach the point where we can query the fundamental and heretofore unquestioned assumptions on which the whole structure of planned change, including who has the right to plan and execute change, is based. Even if we accept the underlying values of contemporary change programs, we find that barriers to change are as prevalent in the structure, values, and operating procedures of bureaucracies and in the personal qualities of the change agents as in the target cultures or subcultures. In fact, sophisticated technical aid specialists, including anthropologists who have worked on development programs, increasingly feel that the monolithic character of bureaucracy constitutes the single largest problem in perfecting the techniques of directed change planning and operation and in defining the moral and ethical criteria on which such planning and operation must be based. It is for this reason that the most exciting future research in applied anthropology probably will involve professional and administrative organizations—their value systems, their structures, their "socialization" processes, and above all, their unquestioned assumptions about their work.

To summarize the last several paragraphs we can say that the best contemporary applied anthropological research should involve equally the twin sociocultural systems of "client group" and "innovating organization" and, of course, the interaction setting, the point at which the two groups come together.

TEAMWORK PROBLEMS

It was stated earlier that an anthropologist is doing applied work when the research problem is selected by someone other than himself and when the research is financed by an organization that has rights over research results and that hopes to use these results in achieving its goals. Obviously, in such a setting the anthropologist interacts with many people from professions quite unlike his own—people who, in more traditional field work, would play lesser roles or be absent entirely. In other words, there is a problem of teamwork: what structural administrative arrangements will insure the anthropologist sufficient autonomy to do what he feels is sound work, to preserve his informants' individual and group rights and freedom, to write up research results—and at the same time, to be useful to the organization with which he is associated, which in all probability has acquired his services because it assumes that anthropological advice will facilitate achievement of project goals.

It has been difficult to achieve a definition of rights, obligations, and expectations that is mutually satisfactory to anthropologists and administrators and technicians working on common problems. This problem is doubtless the greatest stumbling block lying in the way of developing a sophisticated applied anthropology. Much of the problem stems from the fact that anthropologists on the one hand and administrative technical specialists on the other hand belong to distinct professional subcultures where the differences in concepts of roles, of methods of work, of values and goals are far greater than is ordinarily assumed. Both anthropologists and administrative-technical specialists are much more ethnocentric than they realize, in assuming that the norms governing practices within their fields are not only correct and desirable, but also fairly obvious to everyone else. Each assumes that there can be no reasonable disagreement with these norms, which, of course, is far from the truth.

A great part of the problem stems from the fact that while the scientific disciplines, including anthropology, stress theoretical research and contributions to basic knowledge, whether these contributions have obvious practical utility or not, most professional work stresses goal-directed and problem-solving action, which is the raison d'être for a bureaucracy. Predictably, the members of these two different kinds of groups have very different expectations about their proper role behavior, i.e., what they should do, how they should be judged by their peers and by society at large. Usually anthropologists and administrative-technical specialists do not realize how very different these role assumptions are until they find themselves working together in a common project. When either is forced out of his subcultural mold and required to modify his role expectations and behavior a degree of frustration is inevitable.

This frustration seems to be based in considerable degree on the ego-gratifying mechanisms that characterize each field. An anthropologist is judged by his peers not according to what an administrator thinks of his work and not because he contributes to social improvement programs, but because of the cumulative evaluation by anthropological colleagues of his scientific performance, mainly his publications. Similarly, the administrator's judges are his own peers. In a team situation, an anthropologist finds it gratifying to feel that his administrative counterpart or superior rates him highly; the administrator likewise appreciates knowing that the anthropologist considers him to be highly proficient in his field. But both people are playing to essentially different galleries; each must be judged by a different audience. For an anthropologist, even in applied work, his final judges are found in the profession at large. If he is to be judged fairly, he needs time to record the account of his work, applied as well as theoretical. In most applied research, insufficient provision is made for the anthropologist to write for his own colleagues, since writing time at least equals, and probably in most cases exceeds, research time. The administrator wants reports, memoranda, and staff meeting discussions of anthropological findings and insights. Technical specialists in a program need the same type of help. Lengthy and detailed theoretical treatises are of little use in ongoing programs. Few, and possibly no, applied assignments have permitted anthropologists the time they need to write up their research results *for their peers*. Few administrators feel they can so favor an anthropologist over their other staff members, and, from the standpoint of efficiency, even fewer can budget for this kind of time.

This is a basic, and to date nearly insoluble, problem standing in the way of a full-time, highly developed applied anthropology subdiscipline. An ambitious anthropologist who hopes to achieve eminence in his chosen field simply cannot afford to devote much time to applied work, because history shows that few career applied anthropologists have had the facilities to make contributions that their peers consider outstanding. Only when rules of teamwork are developed that permit anthropologists to function as anthropologists, and not as adjuncts to administrators and technical specialists, will a really healthy applied anthropology come into being. Fortunately, we are beginning to see ways this can be achieved, especially in the social science research units that are developing in medical and public health schools. These may well provide the models for further development of applied anthropology.

ETHICS

Applied anthropology implies participation in programs of directed culture change. That is, an organization with staff, budget, and a charge exists to modify in some fashion the behavior of a particular target group of people. Sometimes the target group itself participates in basic decisions, such as when a community taxes itself for better health services, or passes a bond issue for a new and better school system. More often, in the programs in which anthropologists have worked, the decisions are made with little or no participation by the people whose lives are to be changed. Over time the anthropologist's views about the ethics of his participation in directed change programs have varied, and even today there are widespread differences of opinion. In colonial administration prior to World War II, British anthropologists appear to have accepted "indirect rule" and improved colonial administration as legitimate applied activities; it was only after the war, when colonial peoples became more vocal and when the colonial system obviously was breaking up, that anthropologists had serious doubts about the ethics of their earlier work.

Similarly, there has been relatively little questioning of the fundamental justification for the developmental work contemporary American anthropologists have done in health, agriculture, education, and community development. Most Americans, including anthropologists, assume that better health, improved agricultural production, superior education, and communities organized to make their own decisions are goals with which one cannot quarrel. In short, the fundamental assumptions underlying applied anthropology have always been ethnocentric. Only now are these assumptions beginning to be questioned, and it is far from clear what new definitions will emerge.

From the early days of the science, anthropologists have developed and observed an informal, personal code of ethics and this code in general has worked well. It is based on the philosophy that the competent field anthropologist, like the minister or lawyer, is privy to much information that, if carelessly or dishonestly used, can injure his informants. Therefore, the anthropologist alone must control his data and he must use it in such fashion as to protect in every way possible the people among whom he works. Moreover, since the traditional peoples studied by anthropologists have been "simple," i.e., tribal or peasant communities whose lack of knowledge of the world makes it difficult for them to recognize the possible dangers of revelation of data, the anthropologist has a *special* responsibility to decide what might at some subsequent time injure his friends. The anthropological record of protecting informants is good; instances in which injudicious use of research information has harmed tribal or peasant peoples are extremely rare and perhaps altogether lacking.

The emergence of a formally defined applied anthropological field involving teams of people and utilization of data by others than the anthropologist made a generally accepted code of ethics essential. In the United States the Society for Applied Anthropology early recognized this need and it first formalized and published a code of ethics in 1949. This code was subsequently updated and shortened, but the fundamental ideas remain the same. The present code recognizes that an applied anthropologist has specific responsibilities to *Science*—that his work must have integrity and conform to the highest scientific standards of anthropology; to his *Fellow Men*—he must protect their rights and do nothing that will harm them; and to his *Clients*—the organization that is financing his work and will make use of his research results. Most anthropologists feel that the combination personal, traditionally ethical, and formally institutionalized code has maintained a remarkably high ethical standard in the field.

A second type of ethical problem is attracting increasing attention: who has the right to make decisions affecting the lives of other people? Well-staffed specialized bureaucracies in health, education, or agriculture? The major administrative agencies of government? The people who will be affected by change programs? Until relatively recent years it has been assumed that in the programs to which anthropologists have been attached, the basic decisions were to be made by the professional organizations deemed by society to be qualified to do so. Indirect rule? Obviously a decision for the Colonial Office, but certainly not for the native peoples concerned. Health centers in low-income neighborhoods? Clearly the charge of the Department of Public Health. Educational programs and curricula? Educators, of course, have the expertise to make these decisions.

Anthropological opinion as to how such basic decisions are to be made is divided, but most members of the profession feel that the persons who may be affected by a program should play a more important role in planning than has been traditional. Some anthropologists go so far as to argue that "recipient" peoples should be free to pick and choose the ways in which they will change, which kinds of help and services they will accept, and which they will reject. Others feel that in a complex world *no one* is free to pick and choose: the problem, rather, is how authority and decision-making in planned change programs can be structured to minimize injustice, maximize individual freedom, and promote self-decision to the extent possible.

A third type of ethical problem is peculiar to applied anthropology: what kinds of sponsorship can and should an anthropologist accept and what kinds should he reject? During World War II most anthropologists had little or no reluctance to accept employment by wartime agencies, including the departments of defense. In Micronesia, after the war, there appears to have been little feeling that an anthropologist should not work for the navy or for the Department of the Interior. Most anthropologists who have worked for the Agency for International Development have done so with a clear conscience and Peace Corps employment has been looked upon as honorable. But in the midst of a war about which most anthropologists have grave reservations and moral doubts, the whole question of U.S. government employment is undergoing careful scrutiny. Almost all anthropologists feel that it is wrong to use anthropology as a "cover" for nonanthropological ends. Many feel that any research involving classified materials, with consequent restrictions on publication, is not proper for anthropology. A few go so far as to say that since they believe our government is engaged in an immoral war, *all* government use of anthropologists is immoral and that anthropologists should accept no government assignments. Whatever individual views among anthropologists may be on these matters, it is clear that as a profession much more thought is presently being given to the question of what kinds of sponsorship an anthropologist can ethically accept. Indicative of this growing concern was the decision by the Executive Board of the American Anthropological Association early in 1969 that association publications would not accept advertisements for employment involving research whose results cannot be made available to the entire scholarly community through professional channels of communication. The 1969 Annual Meetings of the Association passed a resolution (subject to mail ballot ratification) urging members not to engage in secret or classified research.

THE FUTURE OF APPLIED ANTHROPOLOGY

In spite of the handicaps under which it labors, applied anthropology will grow. Increasing numbers of anthropologists will find careers in medical and public health schools, in education, and in social welfare. Researching the social aspects of technological change will continue to be a major theme and, to the extent that anthropologists can demonstrate a positive as well as a negative attitude towards inevitable change, their counsel in basic planning will become increasingly important. Far more work will be done on contemporary American society than in the past, and perhaps much less on the developmental problems of new countries as these countries acquire their own anthropologists. Certainly the study of bureaucracy, of the innovating and administrative organizations that plan and carry out programs, will increase in importance and some of the most exciting data in the entire field of anthropology will come from this research.

8

ANTHROPOLOGY IN THE UNITED STATES AND ABROAD

In this chapter our attention shifts to the interaction between United States social scientists and the rest of the world.[1] Anthropologists in particular must concern themselves with the relations of social science to the governments, scholars, and peoples of foreign areas because most of the crucial opportunities for research lie outside our borders. The unique potential contributions of anthropology derive from studies of other cultures at other times and in other places. These studies have their own value in illuminating human nature and the human condition, and more specifically, they can ease intercultural relations by increasing mutual understanding. Moreover, without the theoretical insights derived from the study of remote and contrasting cultures our contribution to understanding social problems at home would be severely limited.

FOREIGN OPPORTUNITIES FOR ANTHROPOLOGICAL RESEARCH

Foreign research opportunities are of two kinds: first, those rapidly disappearing tribal societies that can still be studied as

[1] These perspectives were largely contributed by Gelia Tagumpay-Castillo's article, "A View from Southeast Asia," *American Research on Southeast Asian Development: Asian and American Views,* a special report of the Asia Society (New York, 1968).

whole systems interacting with their culturally perceived environments, and second, those regional or national cultures everywhere in the world that are now changing in response to pressures for economic and political development.

The tribal societies are relics of the vast unrecorded periods of human history, before the development of effective long-distance travel and communication and before the growth of dense populations, when men lived in many small, independent, isolated groups. During this time each group developed its own distinctive way of life, carefully adapted over many generations to its particular natural and cultural environment. A wide variety of local customs, social institutions, languages, and world views came into being: in some societies, for instance, men became the ones who obtained the bulk of the daily diet, in others, the women; some groups were almost exclusively vegetarian, others carnivorous; in some societies the entire local group of a number of families lived under a single roof, in others each couple had its separate dwelling, and in still others both man and wife lived separately with their families of birth but visited each other for a while in the evenings; some societies were governed by an autocratic leader, others recognized hardly any difference in individual authority among normal adults; some societies were at peace with their neighbors for generations on end, in others a youth became a proper man only after he had taken an enemy's head. In effect, nature and history made a tremendous assortment of daring experiments with basic human ways of living, which provide precious information about the limits and central tendencies of man's biological and social nature and potential. These natural experiments could never be duplicated in modern civilization, for they were in crucial part dependent on an emptier world than we now have. Moreover, they are experiments that represent the life work of hundreds or thousands of generations of men.

The surviving and rapidly vanishing tribal or "primitive" societies constitute an incalculably valuable fraction of this great array of human experiments in living. The examination of tribal ways of life can not only help tell us how man came to where he now finds himself, but can also help us predict the effects of new social trends and propose solutions to current problems. Where these ways of life are not carefully recorded they become irretrievably lost to the human race.

The knowledge to be gained from research on the reactions of members of various cultures to the pressures of development and modernization is likewise very great. Such studies have barely begun. We have yet to learn which attitudes, institutions, and values are compatible with an urban industrial society; what stages a society must go through when modernizing; and what kinds of change are essential rather than merely the result of historical accident. Such knowledge can only be gained by comparative study of the course of modernization in different societies around the world.

THE ROLE OF ANTHROPOLOGISTS
FROM THE UNITED STATES

The response of United States anthropologists to these opportunities has been to train increasing numbers of U.S. professionals to carry out the necessary research overseas. Unlike many other social scientists, anthropologists have usually gone abroad alone for extended stays. Their experiences in some of the tribal societies have included hardship and danger. The late Allan Holmberg shared the risk of starvation with the Siriono of the Bolivian jungle; Robert Pehrson worked for the Lapps as a herder of reindeer; Raymond Kennedy was killed in Indonesia; others working in a variety of societies have contracted fatal illnesses.

Some anthropologists have enlisted the aid of scholars in the countries where they have worked to gain understanding of the peoples they have come to study. Alfred Kroeber acknowledged his debt to Julio C. Tello in Peru. Junius C. Bird more recently achieved outstanding archaeological finds while working with local people. Robert Redfield carried out his classic work in Yucatan with the collaboration of Alfonso Villa Rojas. On the other hand, many anthropologists going overseas have ignored scholars in the countries where they have worked and in other instances there were no local scholars who knew the societies the anthropologist had come to study. But whether there were or not, U.S. anthropologists have often tended to act as if they were the only ones qualified to carry out the research.

With the worldwide spread of literacy and the development of scholarship and education, foreign reaction to this elitist behavior on the part of U.S. anthropologists has become increasingly critical, especially in the last few years. The events that brought it to the surface have been politically based and are largely irrelevant to the underlying conditions of international collaboration which concern us here. Briefly, in 1964 and 1965 several large-scale projects designed to investigate the factors promoting insurgency in Latin America and elsewhere came to public attention because of the allegation that they constituted preparation for counterinsurgent intervention by the U.S. government. The best-known of these was Project Camelot, funded by the Department of Defense. Such allegations, whether true or not, naturally raised serious questions about the purposes of research by U.S. social scientists in other countries and raised corresponding fears on the part of U.S. social scientists that mistrust abroad would lead to the closing of countries to research by them. It has now become clear that few, if any, social scientists have been formally excluded as a result of these suspected projects. The only countries that are now closed to outside researchers are those that have long been closed for particular political reasons (such as Portuguese Africa, South Africa, and some of the Communist countries) or involved in war.

However, the outcry over the suspected projects has brought to the surface a different problem: resentment by many scholars abroad of the ways in which U.S. social scientists, anthropologists included, have been conducting themselves for many years in their relations with those who are, or should be, their colleagues. Foreign scholars are angry about many things—the apparent or actual use of U.S.-sponsored research to our one-sided politico-economic advantage; the apparent assumption on the part of the U.S. that it has a right to influence social and economic development in other countries in directions not approved by the other governments; inadequate preparation of field workers, particularly in other social sciences; the sheer number of U.S. social scientists conducting apparently well-financed research in their countries, "mining" or extracting data for our own use without any benefit to the host country and possibly to its embarrassment; our failure to publish in local journals and to send copies of reports and publications; exploitation of their students and occasionally of themselves; insensitivity to the customs and values of the country, or utilizing them for our own ends. In several new nations, leaders and intellectuals have resented anthropological interest in their tribal minorities, arguing that emphasis on these groups tends to misrepresent the developmental level of the nation as a whole. In addition, local scholars are offended by our ignoring the work they have done; our implicit assumption that their scholarly traditions are inadequate and that their cultures present obstacles to becoming more like us; and our failure to recognize them as people rather than simply as objects of study.

The regulations on foreign researchers recently issued by the National Research Council of Thailand are symptomatic of what many foreign countries are coming to expect of our social science researchers. These regulations require the filing of quarterly and annual reports on research done in the country and a final report before permission to leave the country is granted. Several governments in Asia are inclined to cooperate with U.S. archaeologists only when they can formulate their own plans to develop museums on the sites of archaeological excavations and to train their own key professionals and technicians with U.S. assistance. Because of such developments, sensitive U.S. researchers have recently been insisting on the importance of establishing relations with colleagues in the country where the research is to be carried out and of promoting the training of students from the country in the discipline.

In order to understand what is wrong in our interaction with our colleagues around the world and what can be done about it, we must first try to understand the causes of their resentment. Social scientists, foreign or U.S., typically invest much time and intellectual energy in studying particular social groups or categories of people. But almost any society, even if it lacks formally trained social scientists, has leaders and intellectuals who have spent a lifetime trying to figure out how certain aspects of their society work and who have often achieved a considerable and subtle understanding. They are likely to wish that they had the resources to support a more thorough study of the group they already know so much about. When a U.S. anthropologist or other social scientist suddenly appears on the scene with comparatively vast funds, the local social scientists find it hard not to be jealous of the "intruder" for attempting to become an "instant expert" in a field in which they had until then considered themselves the principal authorities. This resentment may be increased by the frequent failure of the newcomer to consult the local intellectuals in advance about his research plans, even though often through no fault of his own, and by the inferior position in which the local people are put by their lack of control over research funds, even when they are invited to participate. They may feel that we are repeating mistakes that have been made in earlier work, but in the position we have made for them they can do little about it. They may lack both the money and the opportunity to concentrate on what interests them most and can only find support to work on what interests us, on our terms. It is no wonder that foreign scholars so often politely refuse invitations to take part in U.S.-financed projects. Attitudes based upon such circumstances as these were present in Chile and elsewhere before the fuss over Project Camelot. Camelot was only a symbol that signified to many in the most negative way the consequences of working for the U.S. at the expense of one's own country and oneself.

The kind of American researcher that our foreign colleagues hope for is described clearly by Gelia Tagumpay-Castillo in writing about the various roles U.S. researchers play overseas. One of these, the "idea-stimulator" and "research-facilitator," is described as follows:

> He is a real gem . . . asks the right questions that we may figure out for ourselves what the right answers might be; assists in obtaining research support so that these answers might be forthcoming, and most of all, the research project is ours, not his. The only drawback of this precious gem is that he is such a rare specimen.

Given the desire for scholarly cooperation, the key issue becomes one of competence. This problem is even more complex than those already discussed. Moreover, the question of who is competent applies as much to the U.S. anthropologist as it does to scholars in other countries. Again, unlike some of the other social sciences (not to mention the physical sciences), anthropology depends crucially upon the understanding of many facets of a culture and upon an ability to think in the terms of the culture under study. This is not the end of anthropological inquiry, to be sure, but it is the beginning of any significant contribution. Such competence is not always acquired by the U.S. scientist, even after prolonged residence in another society. Likewise, the non-Western anthropologist faces a comparable problem when it comes to thinking in terms of a science that originated in, and is part of, a very different cultural tradition. The problems of both are somewhat like trying to write creatively in a second language. Fortunately, the parallel is far from complete. If it were we should have had no outstanding contributions from Asian, African, and other non-Western anthropologists and anthropology itself would be impossible.

These considerations suggest, however, that exposure of non-Westerners to the anthropology of the West needs to be very prolonged and intensive or that new anthropologies need to be developed that are more attuned to the content and style of other cultures. Such new anthropologies would of necessity share much or they would not all be scientific. But it would be ethnocentric in the extreme to assume that Western thought has exhausted all scientific approaches. If this were so, we could conclude that the limits of anthropological science had already been reached. In reference to the development of new anthropologies, immersion in another culture and use of another language become, once methodological competence is gained, profound assets and not liabilities. Indeed that is the way U.S. anthropologists have long regarded their own training.

In short, one can see that in their relations with colleagues overseas U.S. anthropologists have for some time been turning opportunities into obstacles. By ignoring certain simple, basic scholarly aspects of their interaction with scholars in countries where they work, they have limited the effectiveness of anthropology as a worldwide discipline. As a further result, U.S. anthropologists are unable to accomplish their full share of the urgent job of salvage anthropology (i.e., protecting archaeological sites and studying promptly disappearing cultures), much less engage in comprehensive comparative studies of development in modern non-Western nations with maximum effectiveness. It is time for anthropologists and the agencies and institutions that support them to reverse this process and to convert what many now see as obstacles into opportunities for collaboration that will greatly multiply the accomplishments of anthropology throughout the world. It is, after all, not the sole U.S. responsibility to salvage the record of unique and disappearing cultures. It is the responsibility of all mankind, the U.S. included. Scientists throughout the world will do the job, if given the support they need and deserve. Nor is it U.S. responsibility to one-sidedly prescribe the course of development in independent and self-respecting nations. We can only hope to learn something about the alternatives for the developing nations if we eschew ethnocentrism and obtain the whole-hearted collaboration of competent colleagues abroad. But this again requires us to provide a share of their support, under terms that we ourselves would accept.

THE WORLD-WIDE DEVELOPMENT OF ANTHROPOLOGY

Throughout the rest of the world anthropology is lagging—in a few cases absolutely, in most cases relatively. For instance, the conclusion was expressed at the last international anthropological congress in Japan that only three countries in the world now have enough resources and personnel to host such a congress in the future: the U.S., the USSR, and Japan. Countries like France and Britain no longer have large enough anthropological establishments to command the resources necessary to invite a gathering as large as the international anthropological congress has become. As in the case of living standards, the gap between us and many other countries has been growing.

One indication of the one-sidedness of anthropology's development is the number of "associates" of the journal entitled *Current Anthropology*. These "associates" are individual subscribers who are teaching or doing research in their respective countries; the subscription price is minimal because of a subsidy from the Wenner-Gren Foundation, and even the minor subscription cost is excused if the person requests it for a valid cause. Hence, apart from political pressures in some countries against personal subscriptions to foreign periodicals, the number of subscribers represents a fair estimate of the active anthropological scholars in each country (see Table 8-1).

The United States "associates" represent some 45 per cent of the total; Japan is a poor second with 5 per cent of the total. Despite the

TABLE 8-1   NUMBER OF ASSOCIATES OF "CURRENT ANTHROPOLOGY"
BY COUNTRY, 1968

Country	Number of Associates
United States	1,287
Japan	150
Germany (East and West)	138
United Kingdom	99
Czechoslovakia	92
France	83
India	82
Canada	68
Hungary	53
Australia	50
Netherlands	50
Poland	49
USSR	47
Others	627
Total	2,875

Source: Courtesy of *Current Anthropology.*

small numbers, some encouragement can be derived from the large
number of countries with fifty or more "associates." The table does
not include "associates" scattered throughout a score of additional
nations. Some countries have no "associates": the Dominican Repub-
lic, Haiti, Bolivia, Cameroon, Rwanda and Urundi, Botswana, Burma
—to mention a few—so that it may not in all cases be easy for the
anthropologist to work closely with native scholars. The USSR figure
is doubtless an underestimate because of constraints against personal
subscriptions; when the International Congress of Anthropology met
in Moscow there were many more than fifty USSR anthropologists
in attendance.

What would be required to mount an effective program of worldwide development for anthropology? In general we would have to
recognize that since a critical part of its subject matter is the diversity
of cultures, the growth of anthropology (and, in varying degree, of
other social sciences) would be greatly aided by encouraging inter-

cultural communication and a diversity of cultural background among its practitioners. Specifically, we suggest several measures. First, and most simply, theses and research reports should be widely circulated in the countries where the research was carried out and, where necessary, translated. Funds for publication and translation of reports on research in foreign areas into the local languages should be regularly requested by project applicants and provided by federal agencies and private foundations supporting research in these areas. Second, large-scale fellowship funds should be provided for graduate students of any country to go anywhere in the world for graduate study. Third, relatively small-scale but crucial support should be made available to allow regional committees of anthropologists to meet, work together, train students, evolve their own developmental plans, and generate support for them from whatever sources seem to them appropriate. Fourth, matching funds approximately equivalent in amount to every grant for U.S.-financed research, including fellowships, should be made available to assist the work of scholars in the countries where anthropologists work, especially those most directly concerned with the research being done by the American anthropologist. Even if this cuts the amount of support available to all U.S. anthropologists, this principle should be established as soon as possible. The most appropriate arrangements to carry out this measure would vary from country to country. In some countries trained social scientists are capable of making immediate use of such funds. In other countries the funds might be used to assist in training persons in social science research.

Obviously much can still be learned about how to promote development of non-Western nations in the mutual interest of all concerned, how to limit explosive growth of the world's population and feed its rapidly increasing numbers, and how to reduce international tensions. We do not claim that anthropology, or even all of the social sciences together, can generate immediate and final solutions to these problems. But anthropology, developed on the world-wide basis sketched here, could make a significant contribution towards finding new ways to meet these problems. And even if it should do less than hoped, the cost of finding out would be relatively minor compared to other items in the federal budget.

If we can achieve this transformation of world anthropology, we can hope to see an increasing relevance of the discipline for achieving the basic goals of the world's peoples. In view of the increasing national and international tensions, the sooner we get at the task the better.

9

ANTHROPOLOGY'S MANPOWER

The growth of anthropology has been spectacular since the end of World War II. Membership in the three principal professional societies, representing the broad spectrum of interests within the discipline, has more than trebled since 1947 (see Table 9-1).

TABLE 9-1 MEMBERSHIP IN ANTHROPOLOGY'S PROFESSIONAL ASSOCIATIONS

Association	1947	1957	1967
American Anthropological Association	1,692	3,656	6,634
Society for American Archaeology	737	1,090	2,036
American Association of Physical Anthropologists	197	429	530

Source: Association records.

The actual number of persons professionally engaged as anthropologists is difficult to determine. Not all professional anthropologists are members of the societies, and the societies include institutional members as well as persons with an amateur interest in the field. The National Register of Scientific Personnel includes 1,219 persons who in 1968 identified themselves as anthropologists.[1] These data are probably underestimates by as much as one-half. It is clear, however,

[1] National Science Foundation, *American Science Manpower, 1968* (Washington, D.C.: National Science Foundation, in press), Appendix Table A-5.

105

that anthropology is a relatively small field, particularly in view of the breadth of its interests.

RECRUITMENT INTO ANTHROPOLOGY

A 1963 survey of faculty members at universities and four-year colleges in the United States revealed that only 24.3 per cent of those then teaching anthropology had decided to pursue anthropology as a career by the end of their sophomore year in college.[2] And only 42 per cent of the anthropology doctorate recipients between 1958 and 1966 had received their bachelor's degrees in anthropology.[3] Anthropologists enter their discipline relatively late in their academic careers. As a result, a particularly heavy burden is placed upon the graduate training program both to introduce students to the discipline and to prepare them for their professional careers.

Since 1962 the American Anthropological Association, with support from the National Science Foundation, has sponsored the Anthropology Curriculum Study Project (ACSP). The purpose of the project has been to encourage the introduction of anthropology into the high school curriculum and to prepare materials in support of that goal. The objective is to reach the largest possible number of students rather than to prepare students for more advanced study. Nevertheless, as these materials become better developed and more widely disseminated throughout the school system in the United States, more students will be exposed early in their education to the intellectual excitement of anthropology, and may, in turn, plan earlier for a career in the field.

[2] U.S. Office of Education, *Teaching Faculty in Universities and 4-Year Colleges, Spring 1963* (OE–53022–63, 1966), Table 15, p. 90.

[3] National Academy of Sciences, *Doctorate Recipients from United States Universities, 1958–1966,* NAS Pub. 1489 (Washington, D.C.: National Academy of Sciences, 1967), Appendix F.

THE BACHELOR'S DEGREE

American colleges and universities awarded 350 bachelor's degrees in anthropology in 1957. By 1967 the number rose to 1,825. The Survey Committee's projections for the next decade suggest that the number of bachelor's degrees to be granted in anthropology in 1977 will be 11,150 (see Figure 9-1). While it is clear that anthropology's popularity has grown considerably in the last decade and that this trend is likely to continue, it is probable that the projection method used by the Committee[4] overestimates the growth of the

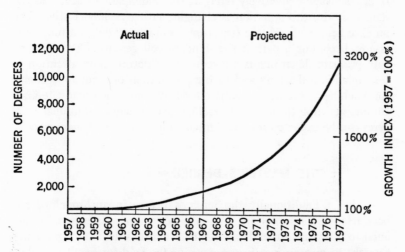

FIGURE 9-1   ANTHROPOLOGY BACHELOR'S AND FIRST PRO-FESSIONAL DEGREES ACTUALLY AWARDED, 1957–67, AND PROJECTED TO 1977

Source: Office of Education for 1957–67 degrees; *The Behavioral and Social Sciences: Outlooks and Needs* (Englewood Cliffs, N.J.: Prentice-Hall, Inc., 1969), Appendix D, for projections 1968–77.

discipline in the decade ahead. Because in the late fifties undergraduate anthropology was taught in many universities in departments of

[4] Described in *The Behavioral and Social Sciences: Outlook and Needs* (Englewood Cliffs, N.J.: Prentice-Hall, Inc., 1969), Appendix D.

sociology, many bachelor's degrees were likely to have been reported in official U.S. Office of Education statistics under sociology. Thus the actual number of anthropology degrees in 1957 may well have been considerably higher than that reported here. This would mean a lower rate of growth between 1957 and 1967 than shown in the figures cited, which in turn would suggest a flattening of the projection curve based upon trends from the preceding decade. While indicating that the data provided here be used with some caution, the statistics certainly demonstrate that undergraduate interest in anthropology has increased considerably in the last decade.

Until fairly recently anthropology has been primarily a graduate discipline, taught relatively rarely at the undergraduate level. As our data indicate, this situation is changing rather rapidly. Rather than an elite field confined to a few strong graduate schools, anthropology is now becoming a part of the standard college curriculum. As a result graduate departments are required to devote more attention to undergraduate teaching and to the preparation of graduate students for teaching at the undergraduate level. As more undergraduate institutions attempt to add anthropology departments, additional pressures can be expected for the limited supply of trained manpower.

THE MASTER'S DEGREE

Traditionally the master's degree in anthropology has been relatively unimportant. When the discipline was essentially confined to a few graduate departments, a master's degree program was thought to give an insufficient grasp of the field for faculty employment. Federal fellowship and traineeship programs, such as those of NSF and NIH, emphasized the support of students seeking the doctorate. Moreover, by limiting the length of support for doctoral study, these aid programs encouraged students to bypass the master's degree entirely and encouraged departments to drop, or deemphasize, the degree. A number of major departments now refuse to admit students whose goal is the terminal MA.

Nevertheless, the master's degree continues to be awarded in increasing numbers. Between 1957 and 1967 the number of anthropology master's degrees increased by five times, from 77 to 357. And the Committee's projections suggest a trebling by 1977, subject to some of the cautions expressed above with regard to the projections of bachelor's degrees (see Figure 9-2).

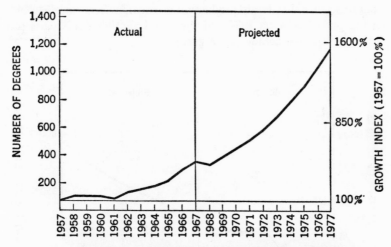

FIGURE 9-2 ANTHROPOLOGY MASTER'S DEGREES ACTU-ALLY AWARDED, 1957–67, AND PROJECTED TO 1977

Source: Office of Education for 1957–67 degrees; *The Behavioral and Social Sciences: Outlook and Needs* (Englewood Cliffs, N. J.: Prentice-Hall, Inc., 1969), Appendix D, for projections 1968–77.

There is now evidence that the master's degree in anthropology is rising in prestige as a consequence of its expanding marketability. Anthropologists at the MA level are needed in smaller colleges and junior colleges and in technical, nonacademic positions in government and industry. Even in secondary schools the MA in anthropology is now more readily accepted as a qualifying degree for social-studies teachers.

With the increasing complexity of anthropological research there will be a growing need for trained support personnel of various sorts. Special master's degree programs might be experimented with to train persons for these tasks.

THE DOCTORATE

Growth in the number of doctorates awarded is perhaps the best measure of the growing research interest and capacity of a field of science. Doctorate production in anthropology almost trebled in the period between 1957 and 1967, and another doubling is projected for the next decade (see Figure 9-3).

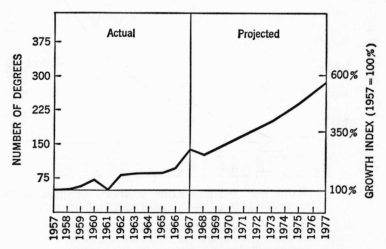

FIGURE 9-3 ANTHROPOLOGY DOCTORAL DEGREES ACTUALLY AWARDED, 1957–67, AND PROJECTED TO 1977

Source: Office of Education for 1957–67 degrees; *The Behavioral and Social Sciences: Outlook and Needs* (Englewood Cliffs, N.J.: Prentice-Hall, Inc., 1969), Appendix D, for projections 1968–77.

In the Survey Committee's questionnaire survey of university PhD-granting departments of anthropology, department chairmen were asked to estimate the number of degrees their departments would be producing in 1972 and 1977. The nineteen large PhD-producing departments that accounted for five-sixths of all of the doctorates awarded in 1967 expect to double their production by 1972, at which point there will be something of a leveling off. The other departments, not now producing many PhD's, but representing 63 per cent of all the departments authorized to award the PhD, expect to increase their production much more rapidly. They estimate that by 1977 they will be producing roughly half of the PhD's in anthropology (see Table 9-2). As will be indicated in the next chapter, these departments will need considerable infusions of funds for faculty, space, and equipment if they are to maintain the standards that exist in the major departments today.

POSTDOCTORAL TRAINING IN ANTHROPOLOGY

The need for continued training after completing the formal requirements for the PhD degree is recognized in all of the sciences, and increasingly so in the social sciences. Approximately 5 per cent of recent doctorates in anthropology secured postdoctoral training upon completion of their degrees, a relatively high proportion compared with other social science fields.

The goals of postdoctoral training are many and varied. A scholar may wish to work with some other scholar whose area of interest overlaps his own; he may wish to develop new skills and techniques; he may wish to learn new languages or broaden his knowledge of other areas of science that might prove insightful in his own work.

Up to the present no form of postdoctoral study, other than the scholar's traditional interest in field research, has found much support in anthropology. Summer institutes, with the exception of the Summer Institute of Linguistics, have seldom been attempted. Their potential value as a means for up-dating the broad core base of the discipline or for carrying the anthropologist more deeply into fields and methods that were not represented in his own training, has never been adequately explored.

There is an increasing need for programs that will offer further training to the postdoctorate anthropologist. Particularly required are specialized training programs to provide surveys of newly evolved fields, of traditional fields that are experiencing rapid growth in data and theory, of new research methods still imperfectly understood by anthropologists and seldom used to their full potential (e.g., methods of computer analysis and statistics), of useful segments of tangent disciplines, and so on. The panel recommends that departments of

TABLE 9-2 ANTHROPOLOGY DOCTORAL DEGREES AWARDED IN 1967 AND ESTIMATED (by Department Chairmen) FOR 1972 AND 1977, BY SIZE OF DEPARTMENT [a]

Size of Department	Number of Departments	Awarded 1967 [b]		Estimated 1972		Estimated 1977	
		Total	Mean per Dept.	Total	Mean per Dept.	Total	Mean per Dept.
Large	19	129	6.8	228	12.0	282	14.9
Other	32	24	.8	175	5.5	284	8.9
Total	51	153	3.0	403	7.9	566	11.1

[a] All figures have been adjusted to correct for failure of some departments to report.
[b] Not all departments granted the PhD in 1967, but all granted at least one PhD between 1960 and 1966.
Source: Departmental Questionnaire, *The Behavioral and Social Sciences: Outlook and Needs* (Englewood Cliffs, N.J.: Prentice-Hall, Inc., 1969), Table 9-6.

anthropology and professional associations of anthropologists develop and seek funding for a series of annual summer institutes to provide training of these types. The panel further recommends that public and private agencies provide long-term support for those programs that prove viable.

WOMEN IN ANTHROPOLOGY

One notable characteristic of anthropology is the relatively high ratio of women to men at the professional level. Given the importance of the intimate relationship between the anthropologist and his informants, there are some inherent advantages in women studying and working with women. A thorough ethnography of any culture calls ideally for female as well as male investigators, with women making especially useful contributions to the study of family life, the process of culture-learning by small children, and the activities restricted to women. In this regard anthropology differs from those social sciences that depend less for their data on an extended close relationship with informants. Anthropology has made wide use of the talents of able women, giving them opportunities to do research and to be heard.

Between 1962 and 1966 20 per cent of all doctorate recipients in anthropology were women.[5] The comparable figure for the social sciences as a whole was 14 per cent, and for all fields of scholarship was 12 per cent.

Many more women who complete undergraduate majors in anthropology might be encouraged to continue for the doctorate if program requirements were liberalized and financial support provided. In addition, fellowship support specifically for the MA degree candidates will assist many married women who find it necessary for family reasons to conclude their formal training at this level. Universities should be encouraged to permit extended leaves of absence without requiring readmission. Rules governing the transfer of credits between universities should be liberalized so as not to penalize

[5] National Academy of Sciences, *Doctorate Recipients from United States Universities 1958–1966*, NAS Pub. 1489. (Washington, D.C.; National Academy of Sciences, 1967). Computed from Table 33.

women who must change their place of residence when their husbands move.

As numbers of women in anthropology increase, it is probable that a growing number of male anthropologists will marry fellow professionals. This presents distinct advantages from the point of view of research, but raises problems for the women with regard to professional employment. Universities are urged to review, with a view toward liberalization, their nepotism rules and to adopt formal maternity leave policies to ensure the fuller participation of qualified professional women in the development of anthropology.

10
ANTHROPOLOGY DEPARTMENTS IN UNIVERSITIES

From 1962 to 1967 the number of anthropology and combined anthropology-sociology departments in the United States and Canada offering the doctorate almost doubled, from 36 to 68. This remarkable growth suggests a substantial increase in the institutional resources available for training advanced students and for further developing anthropological research. In this chapter we will consider the costs of anthropology departments and the funding of anthropological research.

THE DEPARTMENTS SURVEYED

Departments were included in the questionnaire survey of universities conducted by the Behavioral and Social Sciences Survey Committee if they had awarded at least one PhD in anthropology between 1960 and 1966. For purposes of analysis the departments were subdivided into two categories: "large" departments and "others." "Large" anthropology departments were those that produced the most PhD's: nineteen departments produced 84 per cent of doctorates in 1967 (see Table 9-2).[1]

[1] For details concerning the questionnaire survey, and for the list of departments categorized as "large" and "other," see *The Behavioral and Social Sciences: Outlook and Needs* (Englewood Cliffs, N.J.: Prentice-Hall, Inc., 1969), Appendix A. For the list of anthropology departments in the survey, see the appendix to this report.

Anthropology departments, as shown in Table 10-1, tend to be smaller in terms of faculty size than the mean of departments in the social sciences as a whole. Even the "large" anthropology departments fall slightly below the mean faculty size for all fields. In view of the breadth of interests covered by the discipline, departments must, at least under present circumstances, choose between depth and comprehensiveness. These data also suggest the potential advantages that might accrue from the development of regional consortia of university departments, each developing its own specializations to complement rather than compete with the activities of the other departments in the consortium.

TABLE 10-1   PhD-GRANTING DEPARTMENTS IN UNIVERSITIES, 1967, BY SIZE AND FULL-TIME EQUIVALENT FACULTY [a]

Size of Department	Number of Departments	Full-Time Equivalent Faculty	
		Total Faculty	Mean per Dept.
Anthropology			
Large	19	348	18.3
Other	32	326	10.2
Total	51	674	13.2
Six behavioral and social science fields[b]			
Large	132	3,986	30.2
Other	409	6,956	17.0
Total	541	10,942	20.2

[a] All figures have been adjusted for departments in the sample failing to reply.
[b] Anthropology, economics, history, political science, psychology, and sociology.
Source: Departmental Questionnaire and *The Behavioral and Social Sciences: Outlook and Needs* (Englewood Cliffs, N.J.: Prentice-Hall, Inc., 1969), Table 10-2.

Through consortia and similar arrangements, universities are to be encouraged to investigate various ways of reducing costly and unnecessary duplication in such areas as library holdings of important, but little-used research publications; special museum facilities; instructional film libraries; nonanthropological comparative collections maintained for archaeological, ethnobotanical, and physical anthropological use; and research staff support. Space and money saved in this manner may then be concentrated on those special programs in which the university desires professional acclaim, and which contribute most to the strength of the institutional group as a whole. Coupled with this complementarity must go opportunities for graduate students to divide their course work and specialized training among the cooperating departments, thus having the advantage of a wider spectrum of instructional and research facilities. Funding agencies are to be encouraged to support experimental programs along the lines outlined here.

THE COSTS OF A CONTEMPORARY ANTHROPOLOGY DEPARTMENT

Expenditures by anthropology departments for personnel, equipment, and supplies are shown in Table 10-2. The mean cost per faculty member is slightly, but not significantly, higher for the "large" departments. Furthermore, anthropology departments do not vary significantly from the mean for all social science disciplines.

The sources of funds for departmental expenditures are shown in Table 10-3. The university provides by far the largest share—79 per cent—with the remainder derived from the federal government, private foundations, and other nonuniversity sources. Similarly, university sources provide 79 per cent of the total expenditures for all PhD-granting departments in the social sciences.

These data do not include the costs of libraries, museums, separately budgeted institutes, and organized research. Although data are not available from our survey to provide details for these additional expenditures, some orders of magnitude can be obtained. Two per cent of the social scientists in professional schools of business, medicine, public health, and social work at PhD-granting universities included in our survey were anthropologists; the total expenditure for all social science research at these professional schools was $69.3 million in 1967. Thus, on a percentage basis an additional $1.4 million

TABLE 10-2 EXPENDITURES FOR PERSONNEL, EQUIPMENT, AND SUPPLIES PER FULL-TIME EQUIVALENT FACULTY MEMBER, BY SIZE OF DEPARTMENT, 1967

Department	Large Departments		Other Departments		All PhD-Granting Departments	
	Mean Number of FTE Faculty per Dept.	Mean Cost per FTE Faculty Member	Mean Number of FTE Faculty per Dept.	Mean Cost per FTE Faculty Member	Mean Number of FTE Faculty per Dept.	Mean Cost per FTE Faculty Member
Anthropology	18.3	$19,237	10.2	$18,190	13.2	$18,580
Six behavioral and social science fields[a]	30.2	$20,790	17.0	$18,090	20.2	$18,750

[a] Anthropology, economics, history, political science, psychology, and sociology.

Source: Departmental Questionnaire and *The Behavioral and Social Sciences: Outlook and Needs* (Englewood Cliffs, N.J.: Prentice-Hall, Inc., 1969), Table 10-4.

TABLE 10-3 DEPARTMENTAL EXPENDITURES, 1967 (in thousands of dollars)

Department	Number of Departments	Total	General University Sources[a]	Per Cent of Total	Other Sources[b]	Per Cent of Total
Anthropology	51	$ 12,630	$ 10,030	79	$ 2,600	21
All behavioral and social science PhD-granting departments	693	$248,230	$195,720	79	$52,510	21

[a] As assigned to departmental budgets.
[b] Government, private gifts, foundations, as assigned to departments.
Source: Department Questionnaire and *The Behavioral and Social Sciences: Outlook and Needs* (Englewood Cliffs, N. J.: Prentice-Hall, Inc., 1969), Table 10-5.

might be assumed to be devoted to anthropological research at the university level. In addition, 9 per cent of the separately budgeted institutes at PhD-granting universities engaged in behavioral and social science research could be classified as falling primarily within the discipline of anthropology; and certainly other institutes, such as those concerned with the study of certain geographic regions, with language and linguistics, and with developing nations, include anthropologists. If we conservatively assign an additional 1 per cent of the funding of these institutes to anthropology, the research expenditure for anthropology would total $7.9 million for 1967.

COMPUTERS

From computer centers the Survey Committee secured data concerning the use of computers by the various social science disciplines. These data reveal that anthropologists make little use of these devices in their work. Only history, of the other major social science fields, uses them less than anthropology, which accounted for but 1.4 per cent of the total social science computer use.[2]

Although the computer is not yet as widely used in anthropology as in the other behavioral and social sciences, at least *someone* in 82 per cent of anthropology departments uses a computer in his research.

The computer is of great service in linguistics: for example, various kinds of relationships between the units of speech and language may be determined by quantitative methods. In modern archaeology, where fragments of pottery are studied for the interrelationships of their design elements, computer analysis may be appropriate. In physical anthropology various morphological relationships are used in the study of species interrelationships. The more complex the data analyzed, the more likely that the computer will be called upon. Hence an increase in demand for computer time may be anticipated in the years ahead.

[2] See *The Behavioral and Social Sciences: Outlook and Needs* (Englewood Cliffs, N.J.: Prentice-Hall, Inc., 1969), Table 10-6.

SPACE

The need for research laboratories in anthropology makes the field a large consumer of departmental space, second only to psychology among the behavioral and social sciences. Table 10-4

TABLE 10-4 DEPARTMENTAL SPACE, FY 1967, BY MEAN SQUARE FEET PER DEPARTMENT AND PER FULL-TIME EQUIVALENT FACULTY MEMBER

Department	Number of Departments[a]	Mean Square Feet per Dept.	Number of Faculty (FTE)	Mean Square Feet per FTE
Anthropology				
Large	16	16,863	18.3	921
Other	27	6,993	10.2	686
Six behavioral and social science fields[b]				
Large	109	17,113	30.3	565
Other	339	9,448	17.0	556

[a] Actual number of departments reporting on space, not number of PhD-granting departments.

[b] Anthropology, economics, history, political science, psychology, and sociology.

Source: Departmental Questionnaire and *The Behavioral and Social Sciences: Outlook and Needs* (Englewood Cliffs, N.J.: Prentice-Hall, Inc., 1969), Table 10-7.

shows the space presently occupied by departments in terms of the mean per full-time equivalent faculty member. Department chairmen, when asked to estimate their future space requirements, indicated a need for double the 1967 space by 1972, and by 1977 an additional 300,000 square feet over the 1972 amount. Thus over the next decade, assuming a conservative cost of $55 per square foot, the cost of new space for anthropology in already existing PhD-granting departments will be roughly $46.2 million, to which must be added the space costs of new departments to be established in the years ahead.

EQUIPMENT

In terms of the value of present equipment, anthropology departments once again rank second behind psychology in the behavioral and social sciences, but well ahead of sociology. However, anthropology departments seem to anticipate less growth than sociology departments, which appear to see a need in the years ahead for considerably more equipment than they now possess. The data are shown in Table 10-5. Apparently, the major departments will

TABLE 10-5 RESEARCH EQUIPMENT: PRESENT VALUE AND FUTURE NEEDS [a]

Department	Number of Departments	Value in 1967 (Mean per Dept.)	Needed New by 1972 (Mean per Dept.)	Needed New by 1977 (Mean per Dept.)
Anthropology				
Large	19	$74,730	$33,000	$63,000
Other	32	23,000	24,000	46,000
Six behavioral and social science fields[b]				
Large	132	$12,000,000	$ 7,000,000	$13,000,000
Other	409	20,000,000	20,000,000	37,000,000
Total	541	$32,000,000	$27,000,000	$50,000,000

[a] Corrected for missing replies.
[b] Anthropology, economics, history, political science, psychology, and sociology.
Source: Departmental Questionnaire and *The Behavioral and Social Sciences: Outlook and Needs* (Englewood Cliffs, N.J.: Prentice-Hall, Inc., 1969), Table 10-9.

acquire equipment at only half the rate of the "other" departments; however, the "other" departments will still not catch up to the "large" departments by 1977. As the table reveals, the amounts involved in this growth and expansion are considerable.

FIELD COSTS AND OTHER SPECIAL NEEDS
OF ANTHROPOLOGY

The laboratory of a university's chemistry or physics department is customarily located within the walls of the institution and its requirements are readily specified. Anthropology's laboratories are more far-flung. Within the university the laboratory is often associated with a museum, where collections are subjected to study: fossil remains, for example, or artifacts of earlier and contemporary civilizations. Modern methods of age-dating may be applied in such laboratories. But the important laboratories of anthropology are in the field—over the world and especially in those places where Western civilization has had least impact.

Field work is the most costly aspect of anthropological training and research because it so frequently requires travel over long distances, the maintaining of crews of full-time workers who have to be excused from teaching or other duties while in the field, and the transportation of great amounts of equipment and supplies. Because so many opportunities for crucial research on isolated, indigenous cultures are disappearing, it is urgent to secure accurate and detailed records of speech, folklore, and technology (such as agriculture or residential construction). The obtaining of these records requires electronic sound transcribing and colored cinematography. The major budgetary demands of archaeological exploration and excavation are well known. If, therefore, the individual research project in anthropology has a larger proportion of its budget allocated for travel, living expenses, and specially equipped trucks and trailers, this has to be understood in terms of the kind of research in which anthropologists engage.

FEDERAL FUNDING OF
ANTHROPOLOGICAL RESEARCH

Federal support for anthropology has shown a spectacular growth, from $700,000 in 1959 to $11,213,000 in 1967. This increase far exceeds the rate for the social and behavioral sciences as a whole, the funding for which grew from $55 million in 1959 to $296.7 million in 1967.

Table 10-6 shows the principal sources of federal government support for anthropology. Four agencies account for the bulk of this research support—the National Science Foundation, the National Institute of Mental Health, the Smithsonian Institution, and the National Park Service. By far the largest proportion of the research support is for basic research, although the lines between basic and applied research are perhaps so indistinct as to be meaningless.

TABLE 10-6 FEDERAL OBLIGATIONS FOR ANTHROPOLOGICAL RESEARCH, 1967 (in thousands of dollars)

Agency	Basic Research	Applied Research	Total
National Science Foundation	$4,152	—	$ 4,152
Smithsonian Institution	2,267	—	2,267
National Institute of Mental Health	1,285	$1,073	2,358
National Park Service	1,553	—	1,553
Department of Defense	40	578	618
Department of Agriculture	—	143	143
Department of State	—	103	103
National Institutes of Health	18	—	18
Total	$9,316	$1,897	$11,212

Source: National Science Foundation, *Federal Funds for Research, Development, and Other Scientific Activities, Fiscal Years 1967, 1968, and 1969*, NSF 68-27, Vol. XVII (Washington, D.C., 1969), Tables C-26, C-45, and C-64.

PRIVATE SUPPORT FOR ANTHROPOLOGICAL RESEARCH

The role of the private foundation in furthering the development of a field of science is nowhere more striking than in the contribution of the Wenner-Gren Foundation (earlier the Viking Fund) to the development of anthropology. Sizeable resources (although by no means the equivalent of support later secured from the major foundations or from the federal government) were made available in earlier years to the anthropological profession for field work, publication, conferences, education, and other purposes. As a consequence, anthropology grew in stature and came eventually to command larger funding from federal sources. Wenner-Gren financing continues to make possible many professional activities of a special and experimental character not otherwise supported.

This is not the place to trace the history of this support, but it may be pointed out that a major summarization of the field a decade ago—in a large volume entitled *Anthropology Today*—was supported by the Wenner-Gren Foundation. A major international publication, *Current Anthropology*, is subsidized by the foundation, permitting any bona fide anthropologist to subscribe at a price he can afford. The foundation is thus a force unifying the international body of anthropologists as well as providing for specific, otherwise unmet, needs.

Very often a foundation with generous interest in a growing field and an imaginative staff can reap rich rewards for its investment. Anthropologists agree that Wenner-Gren has every right to be proud of its important contribution to the development of anthropology.

11

THE EDUCATION OF ANTHROPOLOGISTS: SOME SUGGESTIONS

In the middle of the nineteenth century when anthropology was emerging as a discipline, the dividing lines between it and other disciplines with related interests were blurred and shadowy. Was Herbert Spencer a sociologist or an anthropologist, or sometimes one and on other occasions the other? As the discipline crystallized and focused on the single organism, man, in all his biological and behavioral variations in time and space, internal foci evolved that led to the four major subfields recognized today. By the 1940s, each subfield had honed its own particular segment of the total discipline to a point so sharp that some feared the dissolution of anthropology as a unified study. There seemed, in fact, to be little justification for the student interested in physical anthropology to develop a familiarity with even the most fundamental data of linguistic or cultural anthropology. Why should the archaeologist, with the vast span of prehistoric time before him, disperse his efforts into other areas of anthropology? And what justification could there be for requiring the cultural anthropologist, with his emphasis on preliterate societies with cultures so remote from the West, to achieve a familiarity with the theoretical structure and findings of sociology?

INTERFIELD AND
INTERDISCIPLINARY INTERESTS

One of the most important trends of the past twenty years, however, has been the emergence of problems that span disciplines or require the merging of two or more subfields of anthropology. This development has not been accompanied by the disappearance of the specialized concerns of the archaeologist or cultural anthropologist; it has been additive rather than substitutive. Anthropology has been reinvigorated by the emergence of these new, field-interlocking problems. The conviction is now strong that, in spite of centrifugal tendencies generated by intense specialization, it must remain a single discipline. Nonetheless, every evidence portends a further intensification of the current blurring of the divisions within the profession in an expanding number of areas, as well as an increasing development of intellectual problems that attract anthropologists with quite different field interests. This creative, dynamic character of the profession has important implications that must be widely recognized by the discipline and that create opportunities upon which constructive action must be taken as promptly and fully as possible.

STUDENT PROGRAM FLEXIBILITY

Curriculum design and graduate degree requirements must reflect these realities. No longer can all students be expected to follow a single training pattern toward an essentially identical goal through much of their advanced program. Anthropology is now too complex, with too many specialities, too great a range of techniques, too broad a knowledge base, and too many areas of overlap with other disciplines. The objective for most graduate students can no longer be mastery of an exhaustive body of facts, concepts, and methodologies across the full spectrum of anthropology. Most, or perhaps all, newly trained professionals should possess a similar broad core of basic knowledge, embracing all four subfields of the discipline. But this requirement must not be so demanding as to prevent its being attained early in the graduate program—by the MA level or, where broad and extensive contact with anthropology has been achieved in the BA program, even earlier. Beyond this point great flexibility is desirable. Students who desire to pursue the more traditional forms of advanced graduate training should be free to choose this option; the advance of the discipline requires some professionals with interests in present problems, including some specialists in general anthropology. But most graduate students must be able to devote the latter part of their graduate period to the acquisition of the deepest possible specialized knowledge about a particular segment of a single field—e.g., the archaeology of the southwestern United States, sociolinguistics, social structure, or human microevolution—and about those still less comprehensive, but relevant, parts of tangent subfields in anthropology and of neighboring disciplines. Knowledge of archaeology, physical anthropology, or linguistic anthropology should be required for the cultural anthropologist only insofar as it serves his particular purpose. Even the traditional foreign language requirement for the doctorate should prevail only when it would advance the student's specific training.

A graduate training pattern of this design will possess substantial merit. Its flexibility should nourish the growth of imaginative, dynamic training programs devoted to particular subfields in the discipline. It should permit graduate training to be tailored to the individual professional needs and interests of the student. It should allow the student to specialize earlier in his graduate work, permitting him to become meaningfully involved in on-going faculty research and to benefit from an apprenticeship relationship. This relationship has proved itself in the biological and physical sciences. It has yet to be widely adopted in anthropology, though it has achieved success in certain research projects in several geographical areas. Sharply focused and intensive training should more fully prepare the student to embark upon his dissertation project and should reduce in scope and duration the graduate program of many well-prepared and highly motivated students. By relaxing the traditional requirement for a comprehensive grasp of the whole field of anthropology and by providing opportunities for students to use their particular competences in their dissertation research, a flexible doctorate program should attract high-quality students from other disciplines. Their highly individual backgrounds and particular skills foster further overlapping of areas within anthropology itself and between anthropology and other fields. The program should produce well trained, specialized anthropologists whose skills and interests are complementary but nonduplicative. Greater flexibility in graduate programs may be expected to stimulate the growth of new interests within the discipline. It should make it less difficult to borrow relevant concepts, methods, and findings from neighboring disciplines. Reducing course contact with the more traditional subjects should encourage students to master research procedures that have been unconventional in the past but are now of growing importance. These range—to take cultural anthropology as an example —from sophisticated statistical methods and computer programming to "exotic" field languages, the administration and evaluation of psychological protocols, and the design and processing of sociological quantitative tests.

It is not intended that the student should be given free rein to plot his course program and his ultimate training goal. It is argued that the present, frequently rigid departmental and graduate school regulations should give way to a more flexible system that will enable the student to develop his professional interests and talents in a sound manner under proper faculty guidance. The student's advisory committee should be given a high degree of freedom, after a core program has been completed, to plan his program and to determine, in consultation with the student, how deeply he should move into which subject areas and how widely he should cast his net. In short, archaeologists—to take this group as an example—should be given the primary voice in determining how much linguistic anthropological training should be expected of an advanced student in archaeology.

THE ROLE OF FIELD WORK IN TRAINING

One of the distinguishing marks of graduate training in anthropology is required field research, usually a basis for the doctoral dissertation. This requirement is most extensive in social-cultural anthropology. Many anthropologists feel that a period of eighteen months is minimal for field work that involves learning a local language. The investigator will probably require several months before he can use the language effectively for interviewing and will need a year or more to approach fluency. Only after he acquires a fairly good linguistic competence can his best field data be obtained.

The field work requirement in the other subfields is usually not as rigorous. A single summer's field research is sometimes considered adequate in physical or linguistic anthropology, and a sequence of two summer projects involving survey and excavation may be sufficient in archaeology.

Anthropologists consider field work an essential part of the graduate training program. Only through personal experience can one fully appreciate and assess the published reports of others, the public data bank of the discipline. Predoctoral field work is also the occasion when much of the research of anthropology is accomplished. Older anthropologists are likely to have problems in leaving their families for extended periods or taking them along to difficult areas and may lack the physical stamina required to conduct field work properly.

Anthropological field work, unlike dissertation research in many other disciplines, tends to be arranged on an individual basis. The anthropologist-to-be (especially the social-cultural anthropologist) does not expect to carve his dissertation out of a professor's research project. Often the student must spend considerable time planning his research and searching for possible sources of support. Once in the field, he is largely on his own. He typically sends back copies of his voluminous field notes to his professor, who can at best sample them, give a few suggestions, and answer a few questions. Even where the latter can offer useful advice, the delay in communications with remote areas usually means that the student must make most decisions on his own.

Field work requirements in anthropology make funds for long-term fellowships necessary, including support for such substantial travel and special research expenses as reimbursing informants, local transportation in the study location, camping equipment, and local shelter. Even with the field trip completed, the anthropology student has a substantial task of writing before him. He will have recorded much more field material than can possibly be used in his dissertation, requiring much time to review the accumulated data, sift out what is relevant to his topic, and organize it into publishable form. In his dissertation the anthropologist is generally expected to do more than simply test a well-defined and logically consistent set of hypotheses. He must observe matters whose existence may have been unsuspected before he began his field research, and he must find some meaning in them. Often items of behavior that seemed inexplicable in the field start to make sense as connections with other intelligible phenomena are noticed, frequently after return from the research location. Ideally such new insights will suggest further questions to ask in the field. For this reason, some anthropologists recommend one or more breaks in the course of field work, to allow the investigator more relaxed circumstances to ponder over what has been learned.

TRAINING INNOVATIONS

We may now turn to a number of problems that may be expected to accompany the departmental and training changes recommended above.

The greater flexibility and freedom in curriculum planning will yield their maximum advantages only if heightened attention is given to the individual student—his objectives, background, and particular educational requirements. This implies heavier counseling loads and more intimate, sustained contact between faculty and student. These goals should be attainable in part through the development of the apprenticeship relationship referred to above. However, increased concern with the student may well require limiting the present largest departments to essentially their current enrollment, increasing the size and quality of the smaller departments, and even encouraging the emergence of new departments of anthropology in universities where appropriate internal support is available.

The graduate program recommended here requires a relaxation of present departmental restrictions to allow and encourage advanced students to include as integral parts of their graduate program a larger number and range of nonanthropology courses. This will necessitate a reexamination of expectancies at least at the doctoral level, a willingness to accept as part of the graduate program relatively low-level courses in other disciplines, and perhaps a broadening of the range of dissertation subjects regarded as acceptable for the anthropology degree. These modifications cannot succeed without correspondingly positive action and cooperation by those departments in which anthropology students desire to take supporting study. The problems foreseen as a result of encouraging students to undertake more course study outside the department are, in fact, particularly those of the other departments. Innovative experimentation is called for to design viable arrangements that will not place unconscionable burdens on these departments. The character of these arrangements will no doubt differ by university, department, and subject. However, a number of patterns suggest themselves:

1. In courses where prerequisites are absent or can be met by most interested anthropology students, standard enrollment requirements may be met. Low-level courses in computer programming, statistics, and sociological research, or psychological projective techniques illustrate this group.

2. Especially in the physical and biological sciences, courses most relevant to anthropology often carry multiple prerequisites. Wherever possible, these should be opened to anthropology students without the full background required of majors, providing they secure the essential technical background through independent reading or tutorials. Grading on a pass-fail basis might often be appropriate. Although such students might be compelled to invest more time and energy for a lower level of understanding than if their preparation were more extensive, the rewards should still be substantial. These should include, with some differences by discipline, a heightened ability to weigh the literature of the field in terms of their own interests, the securing of a basis for further focused study on their own initiative, the acquisition of basic skills necessary for preliminary analyses of data gathered by themselves but relating to the tangent fields, and a recognition of the conditions under which consultative assistance from specialists in the other disciplines is advisable. These are significant competences, particularly because much anthropological research is conducted in the field where the anthropologist must rely so heavily upon his own skills.

3. Where student demand is great and both staff and facilities permit, special courses should be established in the subjects of in-

terest. Such, for example, might be curriculum additions in palaeo-botany, bone identification, and soil morphology, designed explicitly for the archaeologist.

4. Programs of independent study under appropriate faculty or even advanced graduate student supervision should be instituted.

Interdepartmental cooperation is crucial for the success of the graduate program recommended in this report. It is apparent that consortium-like arrangements among geographically close depart-ments of anthropology may substantially ease the burden on other cooperating departments, permitting the pooling of students with similar supporting course requirements. It is equally obvious that, where other departments are generous in their training of advanced anthropology students, anthropology departments must be prepared to offer reciprocal cooperation. Anthropology is convinced that the advance of science will be furthered as much by other subjects borrowing its concepts, techniques, and findings as by anthropology seeking these benefits from other disciplines.

A POSTSCRIPT ON THE FINANCING OF GRADUATE STUDY

In the fall of 1965, only 39 per cent of all first-year graduate students in anthropology received some form of financial aid (other than loans and self-support), as compared with 51 per cent for social science as a whole, 62 per cent for psychology, and 65 per cent for all fields of science.[1] Thus, in addition to the problems of late recruitment into the field noted in Chapter 9, anthropology is not in a competitive position in offering of financial aid.

The situation for students in anthropology vis-a-vis the other social sciences improves beyond the first year, inasmuch as 67 per cent of the anthropologists, as against 68 per cent of social science graduate students, receive some form of financial aid. However, 74 per cent

[1] National Science Foundation, *Graduate Student Support and Manpower Re-sources in Graduate Science Education, Fall 1965, Fall 1966*, NSF 68–13 (Wash-ington, D.C., National Science Foundation, 1968), Table IV-d and Appendix Table B-10. Social science, as used here, omits history and lists psychology separately.

of the psychologists and 80 per cent of all science graduate students receive monetary support.

Given the long period often needed to complete a degree in anthropology and the unusual expenses frequently encountered in conducting field work, anthropology is in obvious need of greater financial assistance for the support of its graduate students. In addition, the nature of the training program makes it especially urgent that fellowships be provided for periods of up to five years without reapplication in the case of students in good standing.

12

SOME RECOMMENDATIONS FOR ADVANCING ANTHROPOLOGY

The needs of anthropology, like those of all other fields of scholarship, include recruiting high-level talent to the field and providing adequate training, followed by support for teaching and research—meaning adequate stipends and salaries, space and facilities, and freedom to move about according to the demands of the area of scholarship. Mobility is particularly important for anthropology, where much of the work must be done in the field, often outside the continental United States. More specific recommendations have arisen from those panel members responsible for analyzing the needs of anthropology's major subfields. Some of their suggestions follow.

REQUIREMENTS WITHIN SOCIAL AND CULTURAL ANTHROPOLOGY

Teachers in Secondary Schools and Colleges

Social anthropology is maturing rapidly. Given the demands of the world today for an informed knowledge of other ways of life and other points of view, we can expect increasing demands for those trained to teach anthropology in both secondary schools and colleges. Anthropologists are already experimenting with curriculum materials for high schools and junior colleges. Some revision will probably be needed in the graduate training program to provide for those who will expect to teach at this level rather than as researchers training other professionals.

There is also a demand for anthropologists to work as technicians in development programs, both in this country and abroad. These must be research people; they may not need the same kind of training as teachers. Some experimentation in planning special programs is already going on and can be encouraged, but the primary need in anthropology, as in any discipline, is for the support necessary for progressive development through continued research.

The Needs for Progressive Development through Research

Help is needed to consolidate the massive accumulation of primary data already available. The first step in this direction will come only with the development of a theoretical base for the interpretation of the data. Funds to provide time free from academic duties are urgently needed. To back up this investment in thought, there should be better training for those already at work in the field and those who are still students. Facilities for the acquisition of certain skills, especially those in mathematics, would clearly repay the investment. Funds for further field research will always be a necessity, though trained professionals should probably today receive funds primarily to provide answers to questions arising from earlier research. Priority should also go to long-term studies where the same populations are followed through time. A number of these studies are already in process and they show that some questions can only be answered by these means.

Training for Field Research and Processing Field Data

Funds for the field training of students might be used to reflect the growing interests of the discipline, for students will always need to be involved in the collection as well as the processing of data if they are to understand the limitations of their work. The data provided by new research create their own demands for clerical and research assistants, program analysts, and in some instances supervisory personnel, if they are to be used most efficiently. The long delay in processing field data is a scandal in anthropology, but understandable enough if we consider the limitations on the time of the man who must at the same time teach and work up massive quantities of data without assistance. Results must be processed quickly. They must be made available to others, which requires the development of quick, inexpensive field reports published in advance of the carefully written formal monographs that only too often are never completed. Financing for special conferences or institutes to facilitate verbal communication of results and the pooling of experience would have some of the same advantages.

Arrangements for Relationships with Foreign Colleagues

One other requirement may be peculiar to anthropology because of its special dependence upon access to other regions of the earth for its research. Arrangements must be made to ease relationships with foreign colleagues. Foreign anthropologists should be able to join with American anthropologists in obtaining funds for projects in their country, in which they would appear as copartners rather than as junior colleagues. It would also be a step forward if foreign colleagues could be assisted in acquiring the training required of American anthropologists. At the present time few of them, even when taking graduate work in American universities, have the opportunity to secure funds for field work outside their own countries. Most available grants are restricted to Americans or to foreign students with resident visas. If foreign students could compete on the same terms as American students for training grants and field funds, some of the bitterness of the present situation might be mitigated and American anthropologists would feel less threatened by the possibility that the regions where they work will be closed to them.

THE SPECIAL PROBLEMS OF ARCHAEOLOGY

In addition to the normal problems of any young and growing science, archaeology has three that are currently of special

concern: the fate of the museum, publication complications, and
the conservation of archaeology's raw material.

Museums

Archaeology, unlike most of the physical and natural
sciences, has not been deeply dependent on the use of complicated
technical equipment requiring large sums of money for purchase
and upkeep. But it has required, and will continue to require, a great
amount of space for the analysis and storage of its basic data. Store-
rooms filled with specimens and the large laboratory tables needed to
examine and process them are two of the trademarks of archaeology.
In addition, the material recovered from archaeological sites has
always been of great interest to the general public and the exhibition
of these items has generated much of the public support for the
discipline. The need for large laboratory and storage space and the
display and interpretation of representative artifacts has prompted a
long and profitable relationship between archaeology and museums.

However, in the academic world museums tend to be equated with
the purely empirical and taxonomic interests of science and with
interest in the object alone rather than the idea behind it. Therefore
museums frequently have difficulty obtaining the support necessary
for their development and continuation.

Although museums and their personnel have traditionally had an
object orientation, just as frequently museum personnel have led in
the development of conceptualization and theory-building in archaeology. Recognizing the importance of the museum for the healthy
continuation of the discipline, the archaeologist must convince others
in anthropology and in the academic world generally that the museum
and its laboratory area provide an essential base for his operations.
Unless he is successful in this endeavor and unless the museum loses
the stigma of being just an object protector the archaeologist will
find himself with a much more difficult problem in filling his
laboratory requirements.

Publication

The need for preliminary reports and for popular summaries written by experts, together with the high cost of archaeological publication, present special problems for archaeology.

No excavation is better than its final published reports. While many excavations lead to such reports, a long time frequently elapses between the end of the field work and their appearance. The paucity of preliminary reports and the tendency to disparage them are regrettable. Progress reports have an important place in all scientific research; even if they are not widely read, they oblige the investigator himself to take stock of his work from time to time. The preparation of a formal statement for the critical eyes of colleagues brings to light gaps in the data and fallacies in interpretation—deficiencies that can otherwise go undiscovered for years. At the same time, the systematic marshalling of facts and ideas will usually suggest new hypotheses and avenues of investigation. More overtly, preliminary reports serve to keep colleagues up-to-date with the accumulation of new data and the evolution of new theories that may be important in their own work. Without them, it is usually necessary to wait a generation or more to achieve any synthesis of ideas arising from the related work of several scholars, undoubtedly why so few syntheses are achieved in archaeology.

Financing the cost of archaeological publication is another problem. A recent review of publication outlets for anthropological writing suggests that archaeologists, like other anthropologists, have no trouble finding publication sources for their monographs, books, and articles. Rather, the journals and publishers have difficulty uncovering well-done and completed works. One of the reasons for this is the cost of preparing and reproducing the necessary plates to adequately illustrate an archaeological publication. Provisions should be made either in research grants or from special funds set aside for this purpose to encourage both a higher quality publication and more rapid completion.

Conservation of Archaeology's Raw Material

The problem of protecting archaeological sites was discussed in Chapter 4, but deserves mention again. The remains of unwritten history constitute irreplaceable treasures. When they are destroyed, human knowledge suffers irreparable loss.

Organization and Financing

Major obstacles to fully realizing the potential contribution of archaeology to the social sciences lie in organization and financing. First, the archaeologist must be supported by organizations dedicated to the conservation of his rapidly diminishing supply of basic data, the archaeological site. Second, he must be supported by organizations that recognize the need to provide the work space, storage areas, and support personnel to handle the data once they are collected. Third, archaeologists over the last quarter of a century have been fortunate to receive a high level of support for the salvage of archaeological material, especially in areas to be covered by federal dams or destroyed by federal highways. However, less support has been available for the pursuit of problem-oriented archaeological projects. Yet it is this type of project that allows archaeology to make its most important contributions to anthropology and to social science generally. Archaeology is expensive because it requires large crews to collect its data, long periods of field time to do an adequate job of collection, and detailed and frequently specialized analyses of a great many bits of data. For archaeology to move ahead on all fronts, each of these factors must be fully understood. In addition, archaeology is presently in an active transitional stage, moving from a strictly empirical to a more theoretical orientation. As a result, support must be made available for the many experimental projects, reflecting this change, that are probing the limits of its data and inferential structure, exploring expanded possibilities for a more sophisticated use of its currently available technical and conceptual tools, and directing attention toward the development of a higher level of theoretical elegance. Only a recognition of these problems and this direction of research will enable archaeology to make its most complete contribution to the science of man.

THE NEEDS AND OPPORTUNITIES
IN LINGUISTIC ANTHROPOLOGY

The Responsibility of the Anthropologist
to Remain Abreast of His Field

The anthropologist who is not primarily a linguist has a responsibility to keep up with his own field. There is a long-range trend in anthropology toward formal analysis, a trend inspired by computer programming, game theory, graph theory, and mathematics proper, as well as linguistics. Different kinds of analysis are appropriate to different problems, but intimate connection with linguistics has made it a major source of anthropological interest and linguistics tends to attract those who have other sources of interest. Moreover, verbal data remain the most successful area of application. In archaeology methods derived from linguistics are beginning to be used in analysis of material culture and style. Knowledge of linguistic methodology is needed to understand results in these lines of research, as well as directly linguistic results like analyses of terminological systems and discourse. The archaeologist also needs some knowledge of methods in historical linguistics to evaluate a language's contributions to prehistory. Also, since understanding the nature of language requires some experience in its analysis, the anthropologist needs linguistic training to study language as part of culture and human language in comparison to communication in other species.

The Need to Record Data That May Be Lost

The field worker has a long-acknowledged responsibility to record data that might otherwise be lost. Much of the anthropological contributions to our knowledge of the world's languages has stemmed from this responsibility. Even lists of words can be useful in placing a dialect or language; accurate texts make possible grammatical sketches. In pursuing his own command of the language, the field worker may gather knowledge valuable to a full grammar, even if he does not undertake its collation himself. There are many problems that cannot be investigated at all without linguistic research and many others for which the quality of the work depends upon linguistic skills. It may be said that linguistic training is a measure of training in ethnography and cultural anthropology, that inadequacy in the former is inadequacy in the latter.

The Need for More Manpower

Linguistic efforts dealing with both current and prehistoric languages are desperately undermanned. At best there is usually only one active specialist in a language; many languages are without competent active specialists at all. Moreover, much of the work done in the past needs to be recast in modern terms if it is to be usable. Since linguistic theory continues to progress, there is continual need for active specialists in each language. Adequate comparability of current results and coordination of research would require a new level of support. In the study of American Indian languages, for example, at least a doubling of active researchers trained in an anthropological context is needed. The next ten years are the last in which most American Indian languages still spoken north of Mexico can be investigated first-hand. And the lack of sustained research on the languages and literatures of the "Five Civilized Tribes" (Cherokee, Choctaw, Creek, Chickasaw, Seminole) should be a cause of national shame. Regional centers or institutes for these and other groups of languages and cultures would be the most effective solution.

The Need for Interdisciplinary Research

There is today a growing need, for reasons of both practical affairs and advance of theory, for linguistic research conducted in the context of the behavioral and social sciences. Mechanical addition of separate skills will not suffice. There is a need for skills oriented from the start along the relevant common lines. The long involvement of anthropology with linguistic research—the tradition of some linguistic training for all students, of work in historical as well as synchronic linguistics, of cross-cultural experience with linguistic diversity, the attention of anthropologists to patterned interpersonal behavior of the sort manifest in language—such things give anthropology a special opportunity, if not a special responsibility, among the social sciences.

Enhancing the Quality of Linguistic Training

As the relevance of linguistic training in anthropology increases, however, the amount and quality does not; perhaps it even decreases. Despite the growth in the number of anthropologists expressing linguistic interests (as shown in the guide to graduate departments), the number of persons available to teach and transmit linguistic skills and to provide models of anthropologically-motivated linguistic research remains quite small. Courses mostly teach about language, not how to do linguistic research. To remedy this situation a department might initiate a two-year sequence of courses in descriptive linguistics, historical linguistics, "language and culture," and field work training. Few institutions offer this training or have the staff to provide it. In the past a single person has trained capable workers, but today at least two full-time specialists or their equivalent (three or four persons sharing linguistic interests) are needed, and must be *mostly or wholly devoted to an anthropology program*. The training cannot be turned over to other programs, for at least three reasons.

First, the relevance of training depends on the instructor. Skills in phonetics and practical lexicography, essential to ethnography and sociolinguistic research, may not interest a theoretical linguist. Second, the most effective way to attain a high level of competence and an understanding of the linking of linguistic and anthropological skills is to mingle students of both kinds of background in common courses and seminars. Third, the kind of linguistics relevant to an anthropologist varies with his field and no single course can be prescribed for all. Within physical anthropology, for example, historical linguistics may be needed by a paleontologist, dialectology by a student of microevolution, and theory of language structure by a student of human evolution and primate communication. Anthropologists must set some of the goals of training if it is to serve their needs.

To meet the needs indicated here, a major expansion, probably at least a doubling, of staff and training in linguistics in anthropology is required. Summer institutes, bringing together the best specialists and students from different institutions, would perhaps give essential impetus. Its long involvement in linguistic research gives anthropology a special opportunity today. It may even be that the future of anthropology as a discipline deserving of independent support hangs more upon its linguistic component than upon anything else. In a time in which the geographical division of labor among the social sciences is disappearing, and sociologists, psychologists, and historians work in Africa, say, as much as anthropologists, linguistic prehistory and linguistic ethnography may be two disciplines that give anthropology distinctive relevance and value.

THE IMPROVEMENT OF
PHYSICAL ANTHROPOLOGY

Better Teaching

At the present time most undergraduate physical anthropology is taught by individuals with little or no training in the field, and the number of PhD's being produced is inadequate to make any major change in the immediate future. Clearly more promising undergraduates should be encouraged to continue their studies at the graduate level. In addition, there is a need for more summer institutes like the one organized at the University of Colorado. These institutes have been highly successful in helping teachers gain an understanding of physical anthropology and physical anthropologists recognize the wisdom of the National Science Foundation in supporting this enterprise for improvement of teaching.

The majority of those who teach about human evolution have not seen the original fossils, living primates, archaeological sites, or the great collections in museums abroad. At present it is very difficult to get financial support for travel for the improvement of understanding and teaching. Yet precisely this sort of experience is needed by those teaching about human evolution and variation. Combined with summer institutes, the provision of summer travel grants for the improvement of teaching would be a major step forward.

Better Laboratories and Facilities

Tradition largely determines the facilities that universities provide for their departments, and no one is surprised that a botany department has laboratory facilities, herbaria, and botanical gardens. Effective teaching and research in modern physical anthropology require comparable facilities. Unfortunately, the narrow "measurement-only" tradition of physical anthropology slowed the realization that the effective study of human evolution, variation, and adaptation requires many techniques and the kind of facilities normally expected in biological science. At present not a single anthropology department in the United States could meet the minimum standard of (1) laboratory space for biochemistry, dissection, and the analysis of archaeological specimens; (2) animal quarters; and (3) storage of specimens. The storage needs are met in some departments that are closely associated with museums, but at present other facilities for teaching and research do not come up to the standard of a second-rate department of anatomy or botany in an American college or university. Provision of more adequate facilities is essential if physical anthropology is to become an effective modern science.

Required Diversity and Enlargement of Staff

Until recently anthropology as a whole was a small field; a department with six or seven members, one of whom was a physical anthropologist, was considered large and adequate. With the advent of departments of fifteen to twenty-five, it has become possible to broaden the coverage in all fields of anthropology. The presence of three or four physical anthropologists, rather than the traditional one, permits the various specialties to be represented, and this should greatly increase the quality of both teaching and research. Not only can no single person master the techniques needed in physical anthropology, but each specialty has links with different parts of anthropology and with other fields. For example, long-term evolutionary studies are closely allied to archaeology, paleontology, and zoology. Short-term investigations involve social anthropology, ecology, and genetics. Primate behavior is particularly related to psychology and ethnology. Increasing the number of physical anthropologists in the new large departments is beginning to allow the science for the first time to move toward a more adequate understanding of man, including both diversity within a department and links with many other departments.

APPENDIX

ANTHROPOLOGY DEPARTMENTS PARTICIPATING IN THE QUESTIONNAIRE SURVEY

University of Arizona
Brandeis University*
Brown University
Bryn Mawr College
University of California, Berkeley
University of California, Davis
University of California, Los Angeles
University of California, Riverside
University of California, Santa Barbara
Catholic University of America
University of Chicago
University of Cincinnati
City University of New York
University of Colorado*
Columbia University
Cornell University
Duke University
University of Florida
Harvard University
University of Hawaii
University of Illinois
Indiana University
University of Massachusetts
University of Michigan
Michigan State University*
University of Minnesota*

University of Missouri at Columbia
University of New Mexico
New York University
State University of New York at Buffalo
University of North Carolina
Northwestern University
Ohio State University
University of Oklahoma*
University of Oregon
University of Pennsylvania
University of Pittsburgh
Rice University
University of Rochester
Southern Illinois University
Southern Methodist University
Stanford University
Syracuse University*
University of Texas, Austin*
Tulane University
University of Utah
University of Washington
Washington State University
Wayne State University
University of Wisconsin, Madison
Yale University

* An asterisk indicates non-response to the questionnaire.